First World War
and Army of Occupation
War Diary
France, Belgium and Germany

16 DIVISION
47 Infantry Brigade,
Brigade Machine Gun Company
(24 April 1916 - 28 February 1918)
and French Mortar Battery
(9 November 1915 - 20 December 1915)

WO95/1971/4-5

The Naval & Military Press Ltd
www.nmarchive.com
Published in association with The National Archives

Published by

The Naval & Military Press Ltd

Unit 10 Ridgewood Industrial Park,

Uckfield, East Sussex,

TN22 5QE England

Tel: +44 (0) 1825 749494

www.naval-military-press.com

www.nmarchive.com

This diary has been reprinted in facsimile from the original. Any imperfections are inevitably reproduced and the quality may fall short of modern type and cartographic standards.

© Crown Copyright
Images reproduced by permission of The National Archives, London, England, 2015.

Contents

Document type	Place/Title	Date From	Date To
Heading	WO95/1971/4		
Heading	16th Division 47th Infy Bde 47th Machine Gun Coy. Apr 1916-Feb 1918		
Miscellaneous	44th M.G. Coy	02/06/1916	02/06/1916
Heading	Confidential War Diary Of No 47 Coy Machine Gun Corps From 24th April 1916 To 31st May 1916 (Volume 1)		
War Diary	Grantham	24/04/1916	25/04/1916
War Diary	Southampton	25/04/1916	25/04/1916
War Diary	Le Havre	26/04/1916	26/04/1916
War Diary	No 1 Rest Camp Le. Havre	27/04/1916	27/04/1916
War Diary	Noeux-Les-Mines	28/04/1916	29/04/1916
War Diary	Philosophe	30/04/1916	02/05/1916
War Diary	Mazingarbe	03/05/1916	17/05/1916
War Diary	Noeux-Les-Mines	21/05/1916	24/05/1916
Operation(al) Order(s)	47 Machine Gun Company Operation Order No. 1	24/05/1916	24/05/1916
Operation(al) Order(s)	47 M.G. Company Operation Order No. 2	06/05/1916	06/05/1916
Operation(al) Order(s)	47 M.G. Company Operation Order No. 3	09/05/1916	09/05/1916
Operation(al) Order(s)	47 Machine Gun Company Operation Order No 4	12/05/1916	12/05/1916
Operation(al) Order(s)	47 M.G. Company Operation Order No 4A	15/05/1916	15/05/1916
Operation(al) Order(s)	47 Machine Gun Company Operation Order No 5	16/05/1916	16/05/1916
Operation(al) Order(s)	47 Machine Gun Company Operation Order No 6	20/05/1916	20/05/1916
Operation(al) Order(s)	47 Machine Gun Company Operation Order No 7	23/05/1916	23/05/1916
Operation(al) Order(s)	47 Machine Gun Company Operation Order No 8	27/05/1916	27/05/1916
Miscellaneous	47 Machine Gun Coy	04/07/1916	04/07/1916
War Diary	Philosophe	01/06/1916	09/06/1916
War Diary	Mazingarbe	10/06/1916	30/06/1916
Operation(al) Order(s)	47 M.G. Company Operation Order No 8	08/06/1916	08/06/1916
Operation(al) Order(s)	47 Machine Gun Company Operation Order No 10	15/06/1916	15/06/1916
Heading	War Diary 47th Machine Gun Company 1st July to 31st July 1916. Volume No. 3		
War Diary	Mazingarbe (Loos Section)	01/07/1916	07/07/1916
War Diary	Philosophe (14 Bis Section)	10/07/1916	14/07/1916
War Diary	Philosophe	15/07/1916	31/07/1916
Operation(al) Order(s)	47 M.G. Company Operation Order No 11	01/07/1916	01/07/1916
Operation(al) Order(s)	47 Machine Gun Company Operation Order No 12	05/07/1916	05/07/1916
Operation(al) Order(s)	47 Machine Gun Company Operation Order No 13	09/07/1916	09/07/1916
Operation(al) Order(s)	47 M.G. Company Operation Order No 14	29/07/1916	29/07/1916
Miscellaneous	O.C. No. 47 M.G. Coy. "S" Battery.	30/08/1917	30/08/1917
Miscellaneous	47th M.G. Coy.		
Heading	War Diary. 47th Machine Gun Company Month Of August, 1916. Volume 5		
War Diary	Noeux Les Mines	01/08/1916	09/08/1916
War Diary	Mazingarbe	09/08/1916	24/08/1916
War Diary	Noeux Les Mines	25/08/1916	26/08/1916
War Diary	Burbure	27/08/1916	28/08/1916
War Diary	Eu Route	29/08/1916	29/08/1916
War Diary	Meaulte	30/08/1916	31/08/1916
War Diary	Montauban	31/08/1916	01/09/1916
Operation(al) Order(s)	47 M.G. Company Operation Order No 15	08/08/1916	08/08/1916

Operation(al) Order(s)	47 M.G. Company Operation Order No 16	23/08/1916	23/08/1916
Heading	War Diary. 47th Machine Gun Company Month Of September 1916. Volume 5		
War Diary	Montauban	01/09/1916	04/09/1916
War Diary	Carnoy	05/09/1916	07/09/1916
War Diary	Briquerie	08/09/1916	10/09/1916
War Diary	Happy Valley Camp	11/09/1916	11/09/1916
War Diary	Vaux	12/09/1916	18/09/1916
War Diary	Marieux	19/09/1916	21/09/1916
War Diary	Meteren	22/09/1916	30/09/1916
Operation(al) Order(s)	47 M.G Company O.O. No 30	02/09/1916	02/09/1916
Operation(al) Order(s)	47 M.G Company O.O. No 31	03/09/1916	03/09/1916
Operation(al) Order(s)	47 M.G Company O.O. No 32	07/09/1916	07/09/1916
Miscellaneous	Operations-3rd September, 1916 App 1	03/09/1916	03/09/1916
Miscellaneous	Operations-9th September, 1916 App. 2	09/09/1916	09/09/1916
Miscellaneous	Remarks on Operations 3rd and 9th September, 1916 App. 3	03/09/1916	03/09/1916
Map	British Trenches N.W. Of Guillemont		
Heading	War Diary Month Of October, 1916 Volume 7 47th Machine Gun Company		
War Diary	La Clytte	01/10/1916	31/10/1916
Heading	War Diary For Month Of November, 1916 Volume 8 47th Machine Gun Company		
War Diary	La Clytte	01/11/1916	21/11/1916
War Diary	Scherpenberg	22/11/1916	30/11/1916
Operation(al) Order(s)	47 M.G. Company Operation Order No 33		
Heading	War Diary For Month Of December, 1916 Volume 9 47th Machine Gun Company		
War Diary	Scherpenberg	01/12/1916	31/12/1916
Heading	War Diary For Month Of January, 1917 Volume 10 47th Machine Gun Company.		
War Diary	Scherpenberg	01/01/1917	30/01/1917
Heading	War Diary For Month Of February, 1917 Volume 11 47th Machine Gun Company.		
War Diary	Scherpenburg	01/02/1917	28/02/1917
Heading	War Diary For Month Of March, 1917. Volume 12 47 Machine Gun Compy.		
War Diary	Scherpenberg	01/03/1917	12/03/1917
War Diary	Piebrouck	13/03/1917	30/03/1917
War Diary	Scherpenburg	31/03/1917	31/03/1917
Heading	War Diary For Month Of April, 1917. Volume 13 47th Machine Gun Coy.		
War Diary	Pioneer Farm	01/04/1917	19/04/1917
War Diary	Klondyke Fm.	20/04/1917	30/04/1917
Heading	War Diary Volume 14 For Month Of May, 1917. 47th Machine Gun Company.		
War Diary	Klondike Farm.	01/05/1917	04/05/1917
War Diary	Pioneer Fm.	05/05/1917	10/05/1917
War Diary	Quarte Croix	11/05/1917	15/05/1917
War Diary	Wallon Cappel	16/05/1917	17/05/1917
War Diary	St. Martin-Au-Laert	18/05/1917	18/05/1917
War Diary	Watterdal	19/05/1917	28/05/1917
War Diary	Longuenesse	29/05/1917	29/05/1917
War Diary	Wallon-Cappel	30/05/1917	30/05/1917
War Diary	Clare Camp. (On Bailleul Locre Road)	31/05/1917	31/05/1917
Miscellaneous	Commanding No 47 M.G. Coy. Appendix "A"	04/05/1917	04/05/1917

Miscellaneous	47th M.G. Coy. Appendix "B"	10/05/1917	10/05/1917
Heading	War Diary. For Month Of June, 1917. Volume. 15 47th Machine Gun Company		
War Diary	Clare Camp	01/06/1917	02/06/1917
War Diary	Klondike Farm	03/06/1917	06/06/1917
War Diary	Chinese Wall (Adv H.Q)	08/06/1917	09/06/1917
War Diary	Klondike Fm.	10/06/1917	13/06/1917
War Diary	Outtersteene	14/06/1917	17/06/1917
War Diary	Locre	18/06/1917	18/06/1917
War Diary	Outtersteene	19/06/1917	20/06/1917
War Diary	Eecke	21/06/1917	22/06/1917
War Diary	Fme Loyswicke	23/06/1917	30/06/1917
Map	47th M.G. Coy		
Map	Appendix "A"		
Heading	47th M.G. Coy. Appendix 1. War Diary June-1917		
Heading	War Diary. For Month Of July, 1917. Volume 16 47th Machine Gun Compy		
War Diary	Zeggers Cappel Area	01/07/1917	13/07/1917
War Diary	Brandhoek	13/07/1917	31/07/1917
War Diary	Trenches	31/07/1917	31/07/1917
Miscellaneous	Programme Of Moves. Appendix "A"		
Miscellaneous	M.G. Force Organization Order. Appendix "B"		
Miscellaneous	M.G. Fire Organization Order. Appendix "B"		
Heading	War Diary. For Month Of August, 1917. Volume 17 47th Machine Gun Compy.		
Heading	No. 47 Machine Gun Company. War Diary For August 1917		
War Diary	Trenches	01/08/1917	01/08/1917
War Diary	Brandhoek Area	02/08/1917	05/08/1917
War Diary	St Lawrence Camp	06/08/1917	14/08/1917
War Diary	Vlamertinghe Area	15/08/1917	16/08/1917
War Diary	Trenches	17/08/1917	17/08/1917
War Diary	Vlamertinghe. Area	18/08/1917	18/08/1917
War Diary	Watou Area	19/08/1917	20/08/1917
War Diary	Eecke	21/08/1917	21/08/1917
War Diary	Bapaume	22/08/1917	22/08/1917
War Diary	Gommiecourt	22/08/1917	25/08/1917
War Diary	Trenches	26/08/1917	31/08/1917
Operation(al) Order(s)	No 47. M.G. Coy. Operation Order No. 1	15/08/1917	15/08/1917
Operation(al) Order(s)	47th M.G. Company Operation Order No 102	25/08/1917	25/08/1917
Miscellaneous	No 47 M.G. Coy. In Operations Of The 16th Unit.		
Heading	War Diary. For Month Of 1917. Volume 18 47th Machine Gun Company		
War Diary	Trenches	01/09/1917	30/09/1917
Heading	War Diary For Month Of October, 1917. 47th Machine Gun Compy. Volume Number 19		
Heading	No. 47 Machine Gun Coy. War Diary. For October, 1917		
War Diary	Trenches	01/10/1917	22/10/1917
War Diary	Ervillers	23/10/1917	31/10/1917
Operation(al) Order(s)	No. 47 Machine Gun Company Operation Order No 105	21/10/1917	21/10/1917
Heading	War Diary For Month Of November, 1917. Volume 20 47th Machine Gun Compy.		
Heading	No. 47 Machine Gun Coy. War Diary November 1917		
War Diary	Trenches	01/11/1917	14/11/1917

War Diary	Ervillers	15/11/1917	17/11/1917
War Diary	Trenches	18/11/1917	30/11/1917
Heading	War Diary, For Month Of December, 1917 Volume 21 47th Machine Gun Company		
Heading	No 47 Machine Gun Coy War Diary December 1917		
War Diary	Trenches	01/12/1917	02/12/1917
War Diary	Gomiecourt	03/12/1917	03/12/1917
War Diary	Beaulencourt	04/12/1917	06/12/1917
War Diary	Tincourt	06/12/1917	09/12/1917
War Diary	Trenches	09/12/1917	15/12/1917
War Diary	Tincourt	16/12/1917	21/12/1917
War Diary	Trenches	22/12/1917	31/12/1917
Operation(al) Order(s)	47th M.G. Coy. Operation Order No 107	20/12/1917	20/12/1917
Heading	War Diary For Month Of January, 1918. Volume 22 47th Machine Gun Coy.		
War Diary	Trenches	01/01/1918	02/01/1918
War Diary	Tincourt	03/01/1918	11/01/1918
War Diary	Trenches	12/01/1918	29/01/1918
War Diary	Villers Faucon	30/01/1918	31/01/1918
Heading	War Diary. For Month Of February, 1918. Volume 47th Machine Gun Company.		
Heading	No. 47 Machine Gun Coy. War Diary For February-1918		
War Diary	Villers Faucon	01/02/1918	06/02/1918
War Diary	Trenches	07/02/1918	28/02/1918
Heading	WO95/1971/5		
Heading	16 Div. 47 Bde 47. Trench Mortar Bty. 1915 Nov To 1915 Dec. 1682		
War Diary	Armagh Wood.	09/11/1915	20/12/1915

woof/557/1971(4)

woof/557/1971(4)

16TH DIVISION
47TH INFY BDE

47TH MACHINE GUN COY.
APR 1916 - FEB 1918

47th M.G. Coy.
44th Infy. Brigade.
B.E.F.
France.

From O.C. 47 M.G. Coy.

To. D.A.G. 3d Echelon.

Herewith original Copy of War Diary together with Operation Orders of this Unit from 24th April, date of embarkation, to 31st May 1916.

J. Beaupré Major
Commdg. No 47 M.G. Coy.

2d. June 1916.

May '16
Feb '18

Army Form C. 2118.

WAR DIARY
or
INTELLIGENCE SUMMARY

(*Erase heading not required.*)

Confidential

War Diary
of
No. 47 Coy Machine Gun Corps.

From 24th April 1916 to 31st May 1916.

(Volume 1).

J. J. Hayes, Major
Commanding

Army Form C. 2118.

WAR DIARY
or
INTELLIGENCE SUMMARY

(Erase heading not required.)

Instructions regarding War Diaries and Intelligence Summaries are contained in F. S. Regs., Part II. and the Staff Manual respectively. Title Pages will be prepared in manuscript.

Place	Date	Hour	Summary of Events and Information	Remarks and references to Appendices
GRANTHAM	24-4-16		No. 4 / 6 M.G. Coy. Mobilised.	
			Officers: Capt. Harper J.S. — Through of company Promoted. Major. 24-4-16.	
			2nd Lieut. Clifford E.	
			" Cregan J.G.	
			" Swaffield J.	
			" Cherry L.	
			" Hadley F.	
			" Dixon O.H.	
			" Williamson A.B.	
			" Nicholls B.	
			" Blackwell G.D.	
			Other Ranks. 143.	
GRANTHAM	25-4-16	5-40am	Entrained.	
SOUTHAMPTON	25-4-16	2-0pm	Detrained.	see
		5-0pm	Embarked on S.S. Courtfield sailed at 7pm.	see
LE HAVRE	26-4-16	4-30am	Arrived	see
		8-0am	Disembarked	
		4-30pm	Left for No 1 Rest Camp.	see

Army Form C. 2118.

WAR DIARY
or
INTELLIGENCE SUMMARY

(Erase heading not required.)

Instructions regarding War Diaries and Intelligence Summaries are contained in F. S. Regs., Part II. and the Staff Manual respectively. Title Pages will be prepared in manuscript.

Place	Date	Hour	Summary of Events and Information	Remarks and references to Appendices
No.1 REST CAMP LE HAVRE	27.4.16	6.0am	Left No.1 REST CAMP.	&c.
		7.30am	Entrained at GARE DES MARCHANDISES.	
NOEUX-LES-MINES	28.4.16	5.0am	Arrived. — Detrained and Billeted	&c.
NOEUX-LES-MINES	29.4.16	6.30pm	Left NOEUX-LES-MINES for PHILOSOPHE. Billeted. Transport remained at NOEUX-LES-MINES	&c.
PHILOSOPHE	30.4.16	9.0am	Reconnoitred trenches. 14. BIS SECTOR.	&c.
PHILOSOPHE	1.5.16		A, B & C SECTIONS went in to Trenches attached to No.35 MACHINE GUN COMPANY for instruction	&c.
PHILOSOPHE	2.5.16		Moved COMPANY HEADQUARTERS from PHILOSOPHE to MAZINGARBE	&c.
MAZINGARBE	3.5.16	6.1pm	Took over MACHINE GUN DEFENCES, 14. BIS. SECTOR from 35. MACHINE GUN COMPANY. A, B & C SECTIONS. D. SECTION took over from No.11. MOTOR MACHINE GUN BATTERY. 14 MACHINE GUNS in trenches 2 MACHINE GUNS in Reserve.	&c.
MAZINGARBE	7.5.16	2.30pm	D SECTION relieved A SECTION who returned to HEADQUARTERS	&c.
MAZINGARBE	10.3.16	2.30pm	A SECTION relieved B SECTION who returned to HEADQUARTERS	&c.

Army Form C. 2118.

WAR DIARY
INTELLIGENCE SUMMARY
(Erase heading not required.)

Instructions regarding War Diaries and Intelligence Summaries are contained in F. S. Regs., Part II. and the Staff Manual respectively. Title Pages will be prepared in manuscript.

Place	Date	Hour	Summary of Events and Information	Remarks and references to Appendices
MAZINGARBE	13-5-16	2·30 p.m.	"B" SECTION relieved "C" SECTION who returned to HEADQUARTERS.	&c.
MAZINGARBE	16-5-16	10·30 a.m.	"A" & "B" SECTIONS with 8 guns handed over to COMMANDANT, LOOS DEFENCES. "C" SECTION relieved "B" SECTION at 65 PT. METRE REDOUBT. 48 MACHINE GUN COMPANY relieved "A" SECTION at GUN ALLEY.	&c.
MAZINGARBE	17-5-16	2·30 a.m.	49 MACHINE GUN COMPANY relieved R1, R2 and "D" SECTION "14 BIS" SECTOR. 48 MACHINE GUN COMPANY relieved R3 & R4 from RESERVE TRENCH "14 BIS" SECTOR. "D" SECTION and 65 PT METRE REDOUBT, I.C. SECTION. Relief completed by 7·30 p.m.	&c.
NOEUX-LES-MINES	21-5-16	7·0 p.m.	"C" and "D" Section relieved A and B SECTIONS at LOOS DEFENCES	&c.
NOEUX-LES-MINES	22-5-16	10·0 p.m.	A, B, C, D Sections relieved 48 Machine Gun Coy. Company Headquarters moved to PHILOSOPHE.	&c.

Copy No 7

Secret   47 Machine Gun Company
         Operation Order No 1.   2nd May 1916.

1. In accordance with 47th Inf. Bde. Op. Order No 28 the completion of the relief of the 35th M.G.Coy and the Section No. 11 M.M.G. Battery in the 14 Bde Section by the 47th M.G. Company will take place to-night.

             positions
2. (a) All guns and stores will be completely taken over from 35 M.G. Coy by 6 p.m.
   (b) 47 M.G. Coy will be responsible for the M.G. Defence of 14 Bde Section from that hour.

3. (a) 2/Lt. Swaffield, 1 N.C.O & 4 men will report to O.C. Section 11 M.M.G. Battery at 4 p.m. today to make arrangements to take over the two gun positions.
   (b) O.C. Section 11 M.M.G. Battery will send two guides to meet the relieving teams at the CRUCIFIX at 8.30 p.m. tonight.

Issued at 10.45 a.m.

Copy No 1	File
" " 2	11 M.M.G. Batt.
" " 3	A Sect.
4	B "
5	C "
6	D "
7	War Diary

J. Sharpe Capt.
Commdg 47 M.G.Coy.

Copy No 6.

Secret.   47 M.G. Company
            Operation Order No 2.   6th May 1916

1. The following relief will take place tomorrow 7th inst
   B Section will take over R1, R2, R3, R4.
   C   "   "   "   "   R5, R6, R7, R10.
   D   "   "   "   "   65 Pt Metre Redoubt.
   A   "   " move back to Coy. Hd Qrs in reserve

2. The ~~Half~~ 2 Teams D Section at present in reserve will take over
   the Redoubt at 2 p.m. at which hour the relief
   will commence.

3. 2 Men per gun will move to new positions
   at 10 a.m. for instruction

4. After relief O.C. A Section will remove guns,
   tripods, spare parts and ammunition from R8 and
   R9 and hand them over to O.C. D Section at
   65 Pt. Metre Redoubt.

5. Relieving sections will proceed VIA NORTHERN
   UP using the entrance 300x of PHILOSOPHE
   RAILWAY CROSSING.

6. Special orders have been issued to O.C. D
   Section re disposal of guns and teams.

7. O.C. A Section will report completion of
   relief on arrival at Company Headquarters.

Issued at 5 p.m.
Copy No 1. A Sec.
 "   " 2   B "
 "   " 3   C "
 "   " 4   D "
 "   " 5. File
 "   " 6. War Diary.

J. Harper Capt.
Commdg 47. M.G. Coy

Secret   47 M.G. Company   Copy. No 6.
           Operation Order No 3.   9th May, 1916.

1. The following relief will take place tomorrow 10th inst.
   C Section will take over   R1, R2, R3, R4.
   D   "   "   "   "   R5, R6, R7, R10.
   A   "   "   "   "   65 Pt. METRE REDOUBT.
   B   "   "   move to Coy. Hd. Qrs in reserve.

2. A Section will take over the REDOUBT by 2.30 p.m. at which hour the relief will commence.

3. 2 Men per gun will report to new positions at 12 noon for instruction.

4. Relieving sections will proceed via NORTERN UP using the entrance 300 W of PHILOSOPHE RAILWAY CROSSING.

5. O.C. B Section will report completion of relief on arrival at Coy. Hd. Qrs.

Issued at 5 p.m.
Copy No 1.   A Section
"   "   2   B   "
"   "   3   C   "
"   "   4   D   "
"   "   5   Filed
"   "   6   War Diary

                                      J. Mackie Capt.
                                      Commdg 47 M.G. Coy.

Secret. 47 Machine Gun Company.
Copy No 6

Operation Order No 4.   12th May 1916

1. The following relief will take place tomorrow 13th inst:
   D Section will take over R1, R2, R3, R4.
   A   "   "   "   R5, R6, R7, R10.
   B   "   "   "   65 Pt Metre Redoubt.
   C   "   " move back to Coy Hd Qrs in reserve.

2. B Section will take over the Redoubt at 2.30 p.m. at which hour the relief will commence.

3. 2 Men per gun will report at their new positions at 12 noon for instruction.

4. Relieving Sections will proceed via NORTERN UP, using entrance 300x W. at PHILOSOPHE RAILWAY CROSSING.

5. O.C. Section to report completion of relief on arrival at Coy Hd Qrs.

Issued at 2 p.m.
Copy No 1. A sec.
Copy No 2   B "
  "   No 3   C "
  "   No 4   D "
  "   No 5   Files
  "   No 6   War Diary

J. Harper Cuff
Comdg 47 M.G. Coy

47 M.G. Company.   Copy No. 6
Operation Order No 4.A   15 May 1916.

1. In accordance with 47th Infy Bgde. Op. Order No 33 the following relief will take place tomorrow 16th inst.

(a) A Section will be relieved at positions R5, R6, R8, R10 starting at 6 a.m. by 48 M.G. Company. On completion of relief A Section will take over 'A' Keep LOOS Defences.

(b) 2/Lt. Blackwell and 2 gun teams will take over 65 Pt Metre Redoubt at 10 a.m.

(c) B Section will completely hand over the Redoubt by 10.30 a.m. at which hour it will proceed to LOOS and take over 'B' Keep with 3 guns, C keep with 1 gun.

2. Receipts must be obtained for all trench stores handed over. Copies of receipts to reach O.C. 65 Pt Metre Redoubt by 9 a.m. 17th inst

3. All work in progress must be carefully handed over to relieving teams.

Issued by runner at 2 p.m.
Copy No 1. M.G.O. LOOS.
 "   " 2. @A Section
 "   " 3. B   "
 "   " 4. 2Lt Blackwell
 "   " 5. Filed.
 "   " 6. War Diary.

J. Barker Capt.
Comdy 47 M.G. Coy

Secret.   47 Machine Gun Company.   Copy No 4
            Operation Order No 5   16th May 1916

1. In accordance with 47th Infy Bde. Op. Order No 33
the following relief will take place tomorrow 17th inst
   (a) R.1 & R2 will be taken over by 49 M.G Company
       at 12 noon.
   (b) R3 & R4 by 48 M.G Company at 2.30 p.m.
   (c) 55 Pt Metre Redoubt by 48 M.G Company at 2.30 p.m.

2. After relief sections will proceed via NORTERN
UP where to PHILOSOPHE CROSS ROADS where
limbers will be waiting, thence to Company
Headquarters MAZINGARBE, where O.C Sections
will report completion of relief.

3. O.C 'C' Section will detail the following
carrying parties.
   (a) 1 N.C.O & 4 men report to R3. 2.30 p.m
       1 N.C.O & 4 men report to 65 Pt Metre Redoubt 2.30 p.m

4. Receipts must be obtained for all trench
stores handed over.

Issued at 5 p.m.
Copy No 1. D Section
"   No 2. C   "
"   No 3. Filed
"   No 4. War Diary.

                                    [signature]
                                    Comdg 47 M.G Coy

Secret 47 Machine Gun Company. Copy No 6.
          Operation Order No. 6. 20 May. 16

1. The following relief will take place tomorrow
   21st inst. at 6 p.m.
   (a) C Section will take over 'B' Keep with
       3 guns – C Keep with 1 Gun.
   (b) D Section will take over 'A' Keep – 4 Guns.

2. All guns, ammunition and trench
   stores will be handed over to relieving
   sections.

3. A & B Sections will return via PHILOSOPHE
   – MAZINGARBE to MONUMENT HUTS at
   NOEUX les MINES after relief.

4. On completion of relief O.C. C and D
   Sections will report to COMMANDANT
   LODS DEFENCES.

Issued at 5 p.m.
Copy No 1. A Sec.
 "   " 2. B "
 "   " 3. C "
 "   " 4. D "
 "   " 5. File
 "   " 6. War Diary.

J. Mayne Major
Commdg 47 M.G. Coy.

Secret. 47 Machine Gun Company   Copy No 7.
        Operation Order No 7.   23rd May 1916.

1. The following relief will take place to-morrow at times stated.

(A) A Section will take over R4, R5, R6, R7 from 48 M.G. Coy. at 10 p.m.

(B) B Section will take over R1, R2, R3, R8 from 48 M.G. Coy. at 10 p.m.

(C) D Section will take over R9, V1, V2, and NORTHERN SAP REDOUBT from 48 M.G. Coy after relief.

(D) C Section will take over 65th Metre REDOUBT from 48 M.G. Cy. after relief.

2. O.C. Sections will hand over all Trench Stores and 10 Boxes S.A.A. per gun.

3. Company Headquarters will open at PHILOSOPHE at 8 p.m. where completion of relief will be reported.

Issued at 6 p.m.
Copy No 1. A Sec.
 "   " 2. B "
 "   " 3. C "
 "   " 4. D "
 "   " 5. O.C 48 M.G Coy.
 "   " 6. File
 "   " 7. War Diary.

                    [signature]
                    Comdg. 47 M.G.Cy

Copy No 6.

Secret. 47 Machine Gun Company
Operation Order No 8   27th May 1916.

1. 'C' Section will take over 1 gun in NORTHERN SAP REDOUBT from D Section at 8pm tonight.

2. After relief the gun of D' section will be withdrawn to TENTH AVENUE in reserve.

3. O.C. 'C' Section will arrange for 8000 rounds S.A.A reserve per gun.

4. O.C. B Section will arrange for a reserve store of 8000 Rds in GUN TRENCH.

5. O.C. A Section will arrange for a reserve store of 8000 Rds in RESERVE TRENCH.

6. S.A.A. to be drawn from Brigade Reserve Store in TENTH AVENUE, 100 Yards S. of POSEN STATION.

Issued at 4 p.m.
Copy No 1. A Sec.
"   " 2. B "
"   " 3. C "
"   " 4. D "
"   " 5. Filed.
"   " 6. War Diary.

J Hayn Major
Comdg 47 M.G. Coy

From O.C.
  47 Machine Gun Coy.

To Officer i/c
        A.G's Office
              Base.

Herewith War Diary for the month of June.

              J Harpur Major.
              Commanding No 47 M.G. Coy

4" July 1916.

Army Form C. 2118.

47. M G Coy

Vol 2

WAR DIARY
or
INTELLIGENCE SUMMARY
(Erase heading not required.)

Place	Date	Hour	Summary of Events and Information	Remarks and references to Appendices
PHILOSOPHE	1st June		Alternative positions for night firing from R3, R6, R7, R9 reconnoitred and put under construction	
	2nd June	10-11am	Positions in Reserve Trench started with S.9 from direction of WINGLES - no damage was done to emplacements.	J.H.
			Night firing positions completed also day firing emplacement constructed at R7. Lines of fire laid to sweep enemy second line and communication trench in H.26.A - H.20.C - H.14.C and PNT 13.B15.	J.H.
	3rd June	9 a.m.	S.9 fired in trench near R4 - 11 of which were duds - no damage to emplacement	J.H.
			Night firing from 9.30 - 12 mn. on above sectors - intermittent shelling of RESERVE TRENCH - otherwise quiet	J.H.
	4th June		Gap in hostile wire 250x S. of POSEN CRATER was swept by R.6 during the night. Firing continued from other positions	J.H.
	5th June		During the day 5 parties consisting of from 3 - 20 men at H.14.C.0.5. and a working party at H.20.H.20.B.0.2. were dispersed by R.7. By night gap in hostile wire reported still open - was fired on all night by R.6. Firing continued from other positions between 10-12 p.m.	
		5.45pm	R7 was searched for with shrapnel - as soon as shelling ceased fire on was re-opened by this gun without drawing further retaliation.	J.H.

Army Form C. 2118.

WAR DIARY
or
INTELLIGENCE SUMMARY

(Erase heading not required.)

Instructions regarding War Diaries and Intelligence Summaries are contained in F. S. Regs., Part II. and the Staff Manual respectively. Title Pages will be prepared in manuscript.

Place	Date	Hour	Summary of Events and Information	Remarks and references to Appendices
PHILOSOPHE	6th June	5am	Trench near R.9. heavily shelled with 5.9. – no damage to emplacement. Few other targets were seen during the day – a working party was dispersed at night by R.3.	F.L.
"	7th June		No night firing possible owing to large working parties on our support line.	F.L.
"	8th June		A very wet night. R.9 and R.6 fired intermittently.	F.L.
"	9th June	9am	GUN TRENCH heavily shelled with 5.9s – no damage to either emplacement. Relieved by 49 M.G. Coy. in the 14 Bde Section. O.O. attached. After relief A,C,O Sections were placed at disposal of COMMANDANT. LOOS. B occupied 65 POINT METRE REDOUBT.	A F.L.
MAZINGARBE	10th – 15th		Nothing to report.	
"	16th		Relieved 48 M.C. Company in the Loos Section. O.O. attached.	B F.L.
"	17th		Night firing arrangements completed at R1, R2, R3, R5 and R7 to sweep communication trenches, roads and Ration Dump at Bois HUGO.	F.L.

Army Form C. 2118.

WAR DIARY
or
INTELLIGENCE SUMMARY
(Erase heading not required.)

Place	Date	Hour	Summary of Events and Information	Remarks and references to Appendices
MAZINGARBE	18th		A quiet day. Night firing continued - good results were evidently obtained on the Dump/ours 10p.m - 11p.m as hostile artillery retaliated with heavy shrapnel on the CRUCIFIX at 11.30 p.m.	FH
"	19th		New night firing emplacement completed at R1. Alternative splinter proof emplacement started at R8.	FH
"	20th	3pm 5pm	Our front and support lines were heavily bombarded - no damage to any emplacement The roads and emplacement in the LONDON ROAD were slightly damaged by a Dud anti-aircraft shell.	FH
"	21st		Emplacement at R8 completed. No night firing possible owing to large working parties in front. 2/L T.G. CREGAN to Hospital. 2/L O.H. DIXON reported arrival from Hospital	FH
"	22nd		A quiet day - night firing again stopped by working parties.	FH
"	23rd		Intermittent shelling over the whole section (cont)	

WAR DIARY or INTELLIGENCE SUMMARY

Army Form C. 2118.

(Erase heading not required.)

Place	Date	Hour	Summary of Events and Information	Remarks and references to Appendices
MALINCAMP	23rd (cont)	8.30pm	Heavy bombardment opened by hostile artillery evidently with a view to doing as much damage to our trenches as possible	
		9pm	Result – nine firing emplacement at R3 blown in – 1 horse shot away. Trench leading to A Section H.Q. slightly damaged.	F18
	24th		In accordance with 184 Div. No A.S. 1213/17 following night firing arrangements were made.	
		11 pm	From R7 Sweeping from H.26.c.5.5 to H.32.a.8.9	
		11.8 pm	" R5 " " M.10.5.1 " M.16.9.0.	
		2 am	" R3 " " N.2.6.2.8 " N.2a.5.5	
		2.30 am	" R1 " " M.13.8.34 " M.10.1.6.	
			Intermittent shelling of Right Sub-section during the afternoon and evening.	F10
	25th	5 am	Positions at R6 and R7 somewhat heavily shelled – no damage was done.	F11
			Arrangements made to support projected raid by from 49th Suff Regt.	
		12 mn	Raid cancelled.	
"	26th		Arrangements made to support raid on front HARTS CRATER – HARRISONS CRATER	
		10.45 pm – 11.45 pm	Bursts of fire on all enemy' communications leading to above front. (cont)	

Army Form C. 2118.

WAR DIARY
or
INTELLIGENCE SUMMARY

(Erase heading not required.)

Instructions regarding War Diaries and Intelligence Summaries are contained in F. S. Regs., Part II. and the Staff Manual respectively. Title Pages will be prepared in manuscript.

Place	Date	Hour	Summary of Events and Information	Remarks and references to Appendices
MAZINGARBE	26th	12 mn	All quiet. Stood to in readiness to support infantry in case of counter attack.	J.H.
"	27th	2.15 a.m	Raiding party returned unmolested.	
			Repairs carried out on portions of trench damaged by previous nights bombardment.	
			Quiet Day.	J.H.
	11 p.m		Fire opened on communications at BOIS HUGO.	
	12 mn		Intense hostile bombardment of right sub-section.	
	12 mn		Gas attack commenced on 14 BIS SECTION, causing bombardment to slacken.	J.H.
"	28th	1 a.m	Emplacement at R2 slightly damaged.	
			No night firing owing to presence of working parties.	
"	29th	10 p.m	Irregular bursts of fire on hostile communications in M12.6 and M12.6 N.R.A-6, Aft. Aft.ft.a. Aft.ft.	J.H.
	12 p.m		R2 silenced hostile machine gun.	
			Slight retaliation opened with heavy shrapnel on R1.	
"	30th		Arrangements made to support attack on TRIANGLE, N. of DOUBLE CRASSIER.	J.H.
			R1 to fire on M12.6.5.4 traversing to M.12.6, 7.6.	
			R2 on communication trench running S.W. S.E. in M11.a.	
			R4 " " " S.E. in M11.G	
			Intermittent shelling throughout the day on our front.	J.H.

SECRET   47 M.G. Company.   A.   Copy No 6.
          Operation Order No 8.   8/6/16

1. In accordance with 16th Div" Op Order No 32, 49 M.G. Company will relieve 47 M.G. Company in the LE BIS Section on the night 9/10 June. On completion of relief 12 guns of 47 M.G. Company will be placed at the disposal of the COMMANDANT LOOS - The remaining 4 guns will occupy the emplacements at present occupied by 47 M.G. Company.

2. After relief
    A Section takesover   A Keep LOOS
    B   "   65 Pt. Mock Redoubt (3 guns)
                     PRIVET REDOUBT (1 gun)
    C   "   B Keep EAST   (2 guns)
                     E Keep   (2 guns)
    D   G Keep.

3. The relief will commence on the morning of the 9th.

4. Section Officers will reconnoitre their new positions (if unknown to them) on the 8th.

5. All ammunition, removed sprayers and trench stores will be handed over

6. All details of day and night firing xxxxx be carefully explained to relieving officers.

7. On completion of relief O.C A,C,D will report to COMMANDANT. LOOS
   All sections will report completion to Coy. H'd Qrs.

8. Company H'd Qrs will move to MAZINGARBE at 7 p.m. 9th inst.

9. Rations for A, C, D Sections will be sent to L&l BARRIER. LOOS

Issued at 10 a.m.

A Harper Mason
Comm'g 67 M.G. Cy

Copy No 1. A Section
" " 2 B "
" " 3 C "
" " 4 D "
" " 5. COMMANDANT LOOS.
" " 6. O.C 49 M.G.Coy.
" " 7. War Diary
" " 8. File

Secret

47. Machine Gun Company. B Copy No 7.
Operation Order No 10.

15th June '16

1. 47 M.G. Company will relieve 48 M.G. Company in the LOOS Section on the 16th inst.

2. A Section will take over R1, R2, R3, R4.
   B   "   "   "   "   2 Guns in VILLAGE LINE
                            2 "   " LENS REDOUBT.
   C   " and 1 gun O Section will take over R5, R6, R7, R8, R9.
   D   " less 1 gun will remain in C Keep LOOS.

3. The above relief to be completed by 6 p.m. with the exception of B Section which will not relieve till 10 p.m.

4. All S.A.A. and trench stores to be taken over.
   O.C. 'C' Section will arrange to send back 40 Belt Boxes per empty ration limbers to Coy. H.Q. on the 16th inst.

5. Copies of Trench Store Receipts to be sent to Coy. H.Q. by 6 a.m. 18th inst.

6. Coy. H.Q. will remain at MAZINGARBE

where completion of relief will be reported by wire.

8. Rations for A, C, & D Sections will be sent to the BARRIER — for B Section to the Dump at the E. end of FOSSE 7 on the LENS Road.

Issued at 8 p.m.

Copy No 1. A Section
" No 2 B "
" " 3 C "
" " 4 D "
" " 5 COMMANDANT LOOS.
" " 6 48 M.G. Coy
" " 7 War Diary
" " 8 File

[signature]
Comdg 17 M.G.C.

July 1/6
47 MGC
Vol 3

WAR DIARY

47th Machine Gun Company

1st. July to 31st. July 1916.

VOLUME No. 3.

Army Form C. 2118.

WAR DIARY
or
INTELLIGENCE SUMMARY

(Erase heading not required.)

Instructions regarding War Diaries and Intelligence Summaries are contained in F. S. Regs., Part II. and the Staff Manual respectively. Title Pages will be prepared in manuscript.

Place	Date	Hour	Summary of Events and Information	Remarks and references to Appendices
MAZINGARBE (LOOS SECTION)	1st July	10.15am / 12noon	Irregular bursts of fire from all guns in RESERVE LINE on hostile communications	
		11.45pm	Night retaliation on R2 and R7 - no damage to guns or emplacements	
"	2nd July	2.30am	During bombing attack on TRIANGLE at M.S.C. and large party of enemy in close order seen from advancing at PUITS 11 N.11.B. Fire was immediately opened from R1 - range 1350 - and the party dispersed - several casualties are claimed.	
			Relieved in the LOOS Section by 4 M.G. Company - after relief 8 Guns (A & D Relns) were placed at disposal of COMMANDANT LOOS. Relief completed at 6.45pm.	A O.O. No 11 attached
"	6th July		A Section relieved by B Section in LOOS Defences D " " C " " " Relief completed at 8 p.m.	B O.O. No. 12 attached
"	8 July		Relieved 48 M.G. Company in the 14 BDE SECTION. Relief completed 5 p.m.	C O.O. No 13 attached

WAR DIARY or INTELLIGENCE SUMMARY

Army Form C. 2118.

Instructions regarding War Diaries and Intelligence Summaries are contained in F.S. Regs., Part II. and the Staff Manual respectively. Title Pages will be prepared in manuscript.

(Erase heading not required.)

Place	Date	Hour	Summary of Events and Information	Remarks and references to Appendices
PHILOSOPHE (14 R/R SECTION)	10th July	12 M.N. to 2.30 a.m.	On accordance with scheme, covering fire was maintained as follows: (a) On communication trench running S.N.E. from H.20.c.5.9. (b) " " N.E. " H.26.a.6.9½.	
	11th	12 M.N. to 1.15 a.m.	(c.) Area of H.20.a was searched. A hostile aeroplane dropped a bomb 20 y from W. portion in CHALK PIT ALLEY. No damage to emplacement.	J.H.
		1.15 a.m.	M.G. retaliation on R.3. from H.25.a. – A fixing traverse was found on this area and hostile gun silenced.	
	12th	1.15 p.m.	Irregular bursts of fire opened for ½ minute on enemy's communications in H.20.a and H.25.a in conjunction with artillery.	J.H.
		5.45 p.m.	Intermittent bursts of fire on HULLOCH – PUITS 13 Road, BOIS HUGO, and tracks N. of BOIS RASE	
		9.45 p.m. to 2.30 a.m.	Somewhat heavy retaliation on RESERVE TRENCH. RIGHT SUB-SECTION.	J.H.
	13th		Quiet Day and night.	
		12 M.N. to 2.30 a.m.	Enemy's communications and RESERVE LINE H.26.a.6.9½ – H.26.a.9.4. searched.	J.H.
	14th		Very quiet Day. Night firing carried out as on previous night. Enemy machine gun active from 9.30 p.m. – 12 m.n. traversing RESERVE TRENCH in RIGHT SUB SECTION and LOOS – HULLUCH ROAD.	J.H.

Army Form C. 2118.

WAR DIARY
or
INTELLIGENCE SUMMARY
(Erase heading not required.)

Instructions regarding War Diaries and Intelligence Summaries are contained in F. S. Regs., Part II. and the Staff Manual respectively. Title Pages will be prepared in manuscript.

Place	Date	Hour	Summary of Events and Information	Remarks and references to Appendices
PHILOSOPHE	15th July		New work was observed on H.14.C. enemy's artillery was opened on this point at 2nd and maintained for 1 hour.	A/A
		9.30 pm – 11.45 pm	Light firing as on previous night.	
"	16th "	9.45 pm – 11.30 pm	Firing carried out on (1) H.20.C.6.9. (2) H.20.a.5.8. (3) H.26.6.5.6. (4) H.26.a.6.9½. Some fire was opened on (3) a hostile M.G. was silenced. Reserve Trench (right subsection) shelled intermittently with 5.9 from direction of WINGLES from 6.30 pm – 8.30 pm. No damage caused to any emplacement.	A/A
"	17th "	9.30 am	Reserve Trench shelled with 5.9 – Shooting indifferent. No damage. Night firing as on previous night. Hostile M.G.s strangely inactive.	A/A
"	18th "		Quiet Day – arrangements completed for supporting infantry raid. Fresh work observed at H.25.a.33 – kept under observation.	A/A
"	19th "	12.30 am 1 am 2 am	R.A moved forward to Boyau 60 fired for 25 mins. on ¾ H.19.d.2½.9½. All guns in right subsection fired on (1) H.20.a.2.1. (2) H.20.c.2.3. (3) H.25.a.81. Right section 45 M.G. Coy co-operated with fire on (1) H.20.a.2.1. (2) area at PUITS 13 Bis. No hostile artillery or machine gun retaliation on any emplacement. Trench Mortar secured for R.A without result.	A/A
"		9.30 pm	Quiet day. Hostile aeroplane dropped 3 bombs, 2 of which failed to explode, about 50 N.W. of V.9. in CHALK PIT ALLEY. – No damage was done. (cont.)	

2449 Wt. W14957/Mgo 750,000 1/16 J.B.C. & A. Forms/C.2118/12.

Army Form C. 2118.

WAR DIARY
or
INTELLIGENCE SUMMARY
(Erase heading not required.)

Instructions regarding War Diaries and Intelligence Summaries are contained in F. S. Regs., Part II. and the Staff Manual respectively. Title Pages will be prepared in manuscript.

Place	Date	Hour	Summary of Events and Information	Remarks and references to Appendices
PHILOSOPHE	19 July 20 p/n	11.50 p/m	Fire opened, as on previous output, in support of infantry raid.	
"	20 July	12.30 a.m	On completion of raid R.A. withdrew to normal position - remainder of quiet continued firing long irregular bursts	
"		1.20 a.m	Cease fire ordered. Rounds fired - 738. Co-operation was arranged with right section 45 M.G.Coy - there was no effective gun on artillery retaliation on any portion. A number of M.G. have undoubtedly been withdrawn from our front.	J.L.
"			Quiet Day. Two officers seen observing and pointing to our line VENDIN ALLEY - BROADWAY from trench at H.19.6.9.5. - Fire was opened from R7 - they were seen no more. Fire carried out on (1) H.20 b.2.1.4. (2) H.26.a.9.4. (3) H.25 c.4.1.	J.L.
"		7.pm		
"		10 pm		
"		12 mn		
"	21" "		Quiet Day.	
"		8.30-9 pm	RESERVE trench (right sub-section) heavily shelled with 5.9 - no damage to any emplacement. Our aeroplanes dropped 2 bombs 50 y.w. of N.9. out of which failed to explode. Night firing carried out as usual?	J.L.
"		2.45 p.m		
"		10 p.m		
"	22nd		An exceptionally quiet day. In support of infantry raid fire opened on areas (1) H.26.a. (2) H.26.c. (3) H.32.a. (4) Bois Hugo (5) communication trench running E. from H.25.c.c.6.14. Cease fire. Rounds fired 6750 Co-operation was arranged with 48 M.G. Coy. 48 M.G.Coy Loo Section and 49 M.G.Coy Hulluch Section	J.L.
"		11.30 pm		
"		1.15 a.m		

Army Form C. 2118.

WAR DIARY
or
INTELLIGENCE SUMMARY

(Erase heading not required.)

Instructions regarding War Diaries and Intelligence Summaries are contained in F.S. Regs., Part II. and the Staff Manual respectively. Title Pages will be prepared in manuscript.

Place	Date	Hour	Summary of Events and Information	Remarks and references to Appendices
PHILOSOPHE	23 July	10 p.m.–12 p.m.	Quiet Day – Hostile M.G. very inactive. Movement noticed at H.31.d.7½.4½. Reported to artillery. Night firing on (1) Dump at H.20.b.7.4. (2) Bois Hugo communications and Dump at H.26.6.1½.	J.H.
"	24 July	7.30 a.m.	Our aeroplane dropped 2 bombs in rear of R.B.q. (GUN TRENCH) – no damage.	
"		12 am – 2 am	Quiet Day – little movement observed. Simultaneous bursts of fire at irregular intervals opened on areas (1) H.20.6. (2) H.26.6. (3) H.26.C. (4) H.26.a. – the Bois Hugo and communications being searched thoroughly – there was no M.G. or artillery retaliation.	
"	25"		Quiet Day Night firing as on previous night	J.H.
"	26 "	8.30 p.m.	Working party observed at H.14.a.6.8½. Work observed in progress on French trench running E. from H.20.a.6.9 – this was thoroughly dealt with at night – also trench at H.31.d.6.4.	J.H.
"		10 p.m. – 12 a.m.		J.H.
"	27 "	10.30 a.m.	Working party observed at H.32.a.2.2 – this point was dealt with at night. Quiet Day – during the night the following points received attention (1) H.19.d.5.9 (2) H.20.b.2.17 (3) H.32.a.2.2 (4) H.26.6.3.1 (5) H.20.a.1.1 (6) H.20.c.6.9.	J.H.
"	28 "		Little observation owing to haze – arrangements made to support raids from right and	

Army Form C. 2118.

WAR DIARY
or
INTELLIGENCE SUMMARY
(Erase heading not required.)

Place	Date	Hour	Summary of Events and Information	Remarks and references to Appendices
PHILOSOPHE	23rd (cont)	11 p.m. 1 a.m.	Text deleted. Fire maintained at irregular intervals on enemy communications.	F.T.
	29th	8.30 a.m. 11.25 a.m.	Small working party engaged and dispersed at H.19.a.5.9 Fire opened in support of Infantry Raid, on enemy Reserve Line and communications in area H.20.a. & H.20.c.	
	30th	5 p.m.	Relieved by 49 M.G. Company. Relief complete 12.30 p.m. Coy. H.Q. opened at NOEUX LES MINES.	O.O. No. 14 attached. D. F.T.
	31st		General clean up of clothing, arms and equipment.	

1/9/16.

A. Marsden Major.
Commdg. 47 M.G. Coy.

Secret

47 M.G. Company   Copy No. 7
Operation Order No 11.   1st July. 1916.

1. 4● M.G. Coy will relieve 47 M.G. Company in the
LOOS Section on the night 2/3 July

2. After relief –
(a) 8 guns will be placed at the disposal of the
COMMANDANT, LOOS.
'A' Section and 1 gun 'D' Section will take over
'A' Keep and position R5 in B Keep.
'D' Section (less 1 gun) will remain in C Keep.
(b) B & C Sections will return to Coy. H.Q.
Gun Limbers will be at FOSSE 7 and the
BARRIER at 11.30 p.m. and 12.30 a.m.
respectively.

3. All ammunition and trench stores will
be handed over.
Copies of receipts to be at Coy. H.Q. by 9 a.m.
4th inst.

4. O.C. 'A' Section will be responsible for the
supervision of R5, B Keep.

5. O.C. 'B' Section will arrange for 1 guide
per team to be at FOSSE 7 at 10.30 p.m.

5. Coy. H.Q. will remain at MAZINGARBE where completion of relief will be reported.

Issued at 10 p.m.

Copy No 1. A Sec
"   " 2. B
"   " 3. C
"   " 4. D
"   " 5. 47 M.G Coy
"   " 6. COMMANDANT LOOS
"   " 7. War Diary
"   " 8. FILED

J. Bagne Major
Comdg 47 M.G.Coy.

B Copy No 6.

Secret   47 Machine Gun Company.   5 July 1916.
                  Operation Order No 12.

1. The following relief will take place tomorrow 6th inst
   commencing at 4 p.m.
   (a) B Sec. will relieve A Sec. in A Keep.
   (b) C "   "   "   D " " ,BC" 2 B) in B Keep

2. All guns, ammunition and trench stores to be handed
   over

3. Route – PHILOSOPHE – NORTERN U.P. – RAILWAY ALLEY –
   ENGLISH ALLEY.

4. On completion of relief A and D Sections will
   return to Coy. H.Q. MAZINGARBE.

Issued at 8 p.m.
Copy No 1. A Sec.
 "   " 2 B "
 "   " 3 C "
 "   " 4 D "
 "   " 5. COMMANDANT LOOS.
 "   " 6. War Diary
 "   " 7. Filed.

                              J. Semper Major
                              Comndt. 47 M.G. Coy

Secret

47 Machine Gun Company.   C   Copy No 7
Operation order No 13.   9th July 1916

1. 47 M.G. Company will relieve 48 M.G. Coy. in the 14 Bde SECTION to-morrow 10th inst. relief to be complete by 9 p.m.

2. B Section will take over R1, R2, R3, & R8a.
   C   "   "   "   "   R4, R5, R6 & R7.
   D   "   "   "   "   R8, R9 & CHALK PIT ALLEY (2 guns)
   A   "   "   "   "   V1, V2, NORTHERN SAP REDOUBT & 65 Metre REDOUBT.

3. Guides will meet Sections as follows.
   C Sec. at JUNCTION of GUN TRENCH - CHALK PIT ALLEY. 3 p.m.
   B "   "   "   "   ENGLISH ALLEY - RESERVE TRENCH 2.30 p.m
   D "   "   "   "   NORTHERN UP - 10th Avenue.   3. p.m.
   A "   "   "   "   "   "   "   "   3.30 p.m

4. All ammunition and trench stores to be taken over. Receipts to reach Coy. H.Q. by 6 a.m. 11th inst.

5. Rations for night 10/11 to POSEN DUMP. POSEN ALLEY, CHALK PIT ALLEY, RAILWAY ALLEY & ENGLISH ALLEY will be closed to down traffic after 9 p.m.

6. Company H.Q will close at MAZINGARBE

and open at PHILOSOPHE at 6 p.m.

Issued at 7.30 p.m.
Copy No 1. A Sec
  "   " 2. B "
  "   " 3. C "
  "   " 4. D "
  "   " 5. COMMANDANT LOOS
  "   " 6. War D: 48 M.G. Coy.
  "   " 7. War Diary
  "   " 8. Filed.

J. Burpee Major
Comm'g 47 M.G. Coy.

Secret.

D   Copy No 6.

47. M.G. Company.
Operation Order No. 14.   29th July 1916.

1. 47 M.G. Company will be relieved by 49 M.G. Company in the 14 BIS Section tomorrow 30th inst, commencing at 10.30.a.m.

2. All ammunition and trenches stores to be handed over - receipts to be at Company H.Q by 9 a.m. 31st inst.

3. 1 Guide per gun will report at JUNCTION of POSEN ALLEY — TENTH AVENUE at 10.15 a.m.

4. After relief sections will return independently to Transport Lines - NOEUX les MINES - Limbers will meet sections at PHILOSOPHE Cross Roads.

5. All sections will be clear of NORTERN UP by 3 p.m. — movement across the open will be in pairs at 100x interval.

6. Company H.Q will close at PHILOSOPHE and open at NOEUX les MINES at 5 p.m.

Issued at 8 p.m.
Copy No 1. A Sec.
"   2 B "

J. Harper Major
Commd. 47 M.G. Cy

Copy No 3. C' Pte
  "   " 4. O Pte.
  "   " 5. 49 M.G.Coy
  "   " 6. War Diary
  "   " 7. Filed,

Appendix "C"

COPY:

To:- O.C. No. 47 M.G. Coy.

Report on Operations July 30 & 31 and Aug. 1st 1917.

"B" Battery.

"B" Battery consisting of "C" and "D" Sections arrived in the Barrage position at DILLY-SWITCH with 8 Guns and all Gun Equipment at 1:30. a.m. 31=7=17.   The Battery left SCHOOL-HOUSE at 10:30.-p.m. but owing to shelling of No. 2 Track took considerable time to arrive in position.

On arrival it was found that all the bed boards for Tripods, Water Cans, Cupolas and ammunition had been broken up and scattered about by enemy shell fire.   All ranks immediately set to work to make new Gun Emplacements, collect water and ammunition and generally re-organize the position.

During this reorganization the enemy shelled the position intermittently, but everything was complete, guns set, aiming posts put out, wire erected behind Gun positions, index boards

Cont'd. →

1

places and sentries posted to warn off infantry, by 3:20.am. 31/7/17.
Enemy shelling increased towards Zero hour, apparently the Barrage Position was fairly well registered.
At Zero all 8 Guns opened fire and continued to fire according to programme until 5:13.am. 31-7-17. One Gun only being temporarily out of action, owing to a near hit by the enemy which caused two casualties. All other Guns fired the whole time and 30,000 rounds of ammunition were expended. Immediately after Zero the enemy shelled BILGY. SWITCH heavily, destroying 10 Belt boxes, & scattering S.A.A. and destroying a pair of binoculars. He also set a Dump on fire at THATCH. FARM in the rear of the position, thereby igniting Very lights and S.A.A.
Guns were dismounted at 5:20am. 31. 7:17, cleaned, new panels inserted, fresh oil, placed in cases and ammunition collected in boxes and bandoliers, ready to move forward
Contd :—

Each man carried 3 bandoliers. Runners were sent to the Group Commander acquainting him with the fact that Guns were in position, also asking for time of move. The telephone was destroyed by shell fire.

The D.M.G.O. visited the Battery at 6:55. a.m. 31-7-17 and advised us to move forward at once.

Immediately afterwards word was received from Group Commander to move forward.

At 7:30. a.m. 31:7:17. "D" Section moved forward under 2/Lt. R.R. SMITH who made for the 2nd Barrage Position between BILL COTTAGE and WILD WOOD arriving there at 9:00. a.m. On arrival Guns were set, and one BELT per Gun was fired. Notification of arrival was sent to Group Commander. This Section fired Barrage as per programme.

"C" Section under Lt. R.J. WEBB immediately followed "D" but owing to an exceptionally heavy

cont →

heavy barrage on Wild Wood, had to take up a position on the right of the railway.

Waited at first barrage position until all was clear and then caught up "C" section and lead them up to 2nd Barrage Position.

At this position we sustained two casualties and had one bipod and some spare parts bar ???shafts.

Only six Guns fires, one - having become detached and one having lost bipod. 9,000 rounds were fired.

As per Programme we moved forward to the final barrage position at 10:45 a.m. 31-7-17. "D" Section arriving at 11:45 a.m. and "C" Section at 12:00 - mid-day.

Owing to heavy shell fire "D" Section had to retire to a position 200ˣ in rear of programme position where they remained until they moved out of the line at 5 p.m. 31:7:17. New Quadrant Elevations were worked out, and Guns set for S.O.S. barrage.

over →

"C" Section arrives with 3 Guns which were mounted as per programme and set for the S.O.S. barrage.

The situation at this 3rd position seemed moderately quiet until 6:00.p.m. when an enemy aeroplane flew along the barrage line at a height of 200 or 300 feet.

Following this plane came heavy shelling of the position but Guns remained intact.

The Gun detached from #1 R.R. SMITH arrives here at 5:00.p.m. but without tripod.

At 6:45 p.m. part of the line (20 men) in front broke and came running back to this barrage line. I immediately ordered the 3 Guns to open fire on the S.O.S. barrage & continued firing for an hour.

We arrived at this position with 6 belts boxes per Gun and 2,500 rounds in bandoliers but we collected ammunition

Cont →

four wounded soldiers and a disabled Lewis Gun Team, altogether firing 10,000 rounds.

At 7:45 p.m. the infantry who had retired returned to their original line in front of Damage Position, and everything seemed normal. I removed my Guns at 8:00 p.m. on 31:7:17. I reported to the Group Commander at WILD-WOOD. at 8:30. p.m. on my way out of the line. He then informed me that an order had just come through that all Guns must stay, and that I must take up a position in front of Bile Cottage and dig myself in, making a strong point.

One Gun was lent to the Group Commander and I took the remainder to the position stated.

Here we selected a position 300 yards in rear of some barbed wire and 150 yards in front

contd ⟶

of BILL COTTAGE. A trench was dug and Gun Emplacements made. Six boxes of ammunition were obtained per Gun from the Group Commander and we took up our position, remaining throughout the night and until 2:30 p.m. 1=8=17.

Enemy was quiet throughout the night and during the morning until 11:00 a.m. when he shelled the line from WILD WOOD to BILL COTTAGE very heavily.

Owing to rain the trench became knee-deep in water and the sides caved in, giving little cover to the men and causing considerable difficulty in keeping the Guns in position and ammunition clean.

At 2:00 p.m. I had one Gun and all equipment completely knocked out and 5 casualties

At 2:30 p.m. the D.M.G.O. ordered me to move out — this we accomplished with one more casualty — Onto →

Loss of time in getting to the final position was caused by casualties, weakness of Gun Teams from the beginning, but mainly through having no carrying parties attached.

Shortage of Ammunition at the final position was caused by not being able to pick up the mules owing to their not being able to get up to their appointed dumping place.

Twice during the action Teams came under Enemy M.G. fire viz:- In getting from No.2 Barrage Position to the final position, and when in the strong point in front of BILL COTTAGE.

All N.C.Os. and men behaved splendidly, especially those who remained in the strong point during 12 hours heavy rain.

Cont'd →

I should like to mention Lt. R. R. SMITH who carried out the programme thoroughly, although detached from me, he had only joined us the day before the engagement and had not been in this part of the line or over the ground.

Of other ranks, Sgt TISDALL who, though wounded in the face, at the commencement of the action carried on until the finish.

Geo. H. Merry. Lieut.
47 M. G. Coy.
1/ch B Batton.

To O.C. Appendix "D"
4th M.G. Coy.

Offensive Operations 31st July 1917

The Coy, Company M.B. Sections, attached to 13th Division left Camp at 6.45 pm on the evening of the 30th up to 8 preceded by C. section and march to the LONGE YPRES.

Guns, Tripods, Spare parts etc were picked up here & the Sections then moved off by KRUIT LANE, HALF MOON TRENCH, WARWICK L.R. to C battery position at I.30.a.15.13.

On arrival it was found that S.H.H. dump had been blown up, as had also the dugout containing the reserve belt boxes. Work was immediately begun & the battery divided into two groups, under Lts & Stokes & Brewer & Lt Wallace.

Emplacements were made in shell holes among dead put out, and erected in rear of each group. Sentries on the line & [illeg] for [illeg] & Lewis [illeg] officer.

At Zero hour guns opened fire on target:—
    C.30.d.1.90. To C.30.a.94.08 & continued firing until end Zero +10 am.

At Zero +19 all Guns elevated to target:—
    D.25.a.40.00 to D.25.a.15.54. & continued to fire on this target until Zero +15 am, searching fire being used up to 400'-500' beyond target. During this period 10k was killed & 5 wounded, 1 Gun destroyed by direct hit

At 11.0 am all Guns registered on 1 Target.

D.03.6.15. a.p. to D.19.0.15.a.p. again being the limits, continued on all occasions. During this period 1 NCO & 1 [?] wounded & two damaged, this was expected owing to 5 to action. The firing was heavy [?] all the time & great difficulty was experienced in :–

    1. Getting into position
    2. Laying a line for lock-filling machine
    3. Keeping up the supply of ammunition, owing to heavy rifle & [?] fire directed on the W.S Sea Falls.

The total no. of rounds fired during the course of the first barrage was 3000 rounds.

The [?] discharge of [?] bullets could not be strictly adhered to owing to [?] of guns being put out of action.

The battery came into action with an average of 1 Non. & 1 O.R. per team, [?] [?] casualties were [?] [?] the team came to move forward great difficulty was experienced in getting up sufficient ammunition. There was hardly enough [?] efforts to be made forward every [?] to be taken.

The battery moved off from its position at F.S.C.15.15. at three & 4 yds were cut forward parallel to the Pozières–Bazentin road & [?] [?] taken up [?] [?] [?] that [?] [?] [?] [?] [?] road was being heavily shelled.

(3)

The position eventually occupied by the battery was:-
C.30.b.6.2. During this move 1 O.R. was killed & 2 O.R. wounded.
Positions were once taken up in shell holes & no further move
made, One belt per Gun was fired as soon as everything
was ready. The ammunition supply was very short,
amounting to 2 boxes per Gun & about 30 bandoliers.
A certain amount of S.A.A. was collected from the Infantry
& Wounded, this enabled the barrage programme to be
carried on & a reserve of 2 boxes per Gun was kept in
hand.

A N.C.O. & four men were sent for S.A.A. this party did
not return, four being wounded & one losing himself.
During the whole time the battery was in this position
they were heavily shelled, due I think to the fact
that an Enemy Aeroplane came over at a very low
height & observed the position.

It here +/ the battery moved forward, but owing to:-
1. The heavy barrage put down by the enemy
   in the line between SQUARE Fm. and
   FREZENBERG.
2. The uncertain report received from Bell
   Hill as regards the actual line held by our
   own troops & shortage of ammunition I decided
   to take up a position about C.30.b.8.1.

It here +/39 the battery fired on target
D.21.c.08.24. To D.15.c.88.60.

Having no ammunition & being unable to obtain any at 1010 & 1910. I withdrew the remainder of the Battery reported at the EOOHE here at 11.50.

———————————————

Observation

A carrying party is absolutely necessary if the Lett Batt. is to be without it. In this case practically no ammunition could be obtained & it was only with great difficulty that a small amount of firing was carried out.

———————————————

WAR DIARY.

47th Machine Gun Company

MONTH OF AUGUST, 1916.

VOLUME:-

Army Form C. 2118.

WAR DIARY
or
INTELLIGENCE SUMMARY

(Erase heading not required.)

Instructions regarding War Diaries and Intelligence Summaries are contained in F. S. Regs., Part II. and the Staff Manual respectively. Title Pages will be prepared in manuscript.

Place	Date	Hour	Summary of Events and Information	Remarks and references to Appendices
NOEUX les MINES	1st Aug to 8th Aug		In Divisional Reserve. Daily programme of training, route marching &c. carried out.	F.H.
MAZINGARBE	9th	12 noon	Relieved the 120 M.G. Company in LOOS Section. 2/Lt E. CLIFFORD evacuated (SICK).	F.H. D.O.No 1st attached Marked A
	10th		Quiet day and night.	
		1am-2am	ENCLOSURE AVENUE was shelled with 4.2". No damage done to any emplacement.	F.H.
		10 p.m -12:30am	All quiet fired intermittently on hostile communications - particular attention being paid to dumps at M.12.b.4.4.	F.H.
	11th	2 am /10pm	Enclosure Avenue shelled for 1 hour with 7.5 mm VERY MINE - no damage. otherwise quiet generally.	F.H.
	12th	9:30pm 12am	Beyond usual shelling of ENCLOSURE AVENUE nothing to report. Indirect fire carried out on hostile dumps and communications.	F.H.
	13th	3 p.m.	House at R.4 received a direct hit from 7.5mm - emplacement slightly damaged. otherwise quiet	F.H.
	14th	5 p.m 6 p.m	R.6 and Left Section R.P. treated with Shrapnel - no damage. Very quiet night.	F.H.
	15th		Slightly increased M.G. activity at night - all positions were shelled with shrapnel in retaliation for our french mortar fire. Lt D.C. Kennedy reported arrival on appointment	F.H.

2449 Wt. W14957/M90 750,000 1/16 J.B.C. & A. Forms/C.2118/12.

Army Form C. 2118.

WAR DIARY
or
INTELLIGENCE SUMMARY
(Erase heading not required.)

Place	Date	Hour	Summary of Events and Information	Remarks and references to Appendices
MAZINGARBE	17th	4.30 a.m 10 p.m	Major meeting of ruin line - otherwise quiet. Night firing as usual	F.16
"	18th	2 a.m	Vicinity R.E. heavily shelled with 5.9. - no damage was done. Usual shelling during the day	F.16
"	19th		Quiet day	
		9-9.40pm	A bombardment carried out on left sub-section - no attack followed.	
		3.45 p.m	In conjunction with artillery bombardment guns fired as follows:- (1) M.12.6.4½.4 traversing to M.12.6.9.7 (2) M.12.6.9.7 traversing to M.12.6.4½.4. (3) M.11.6.1.8. (4) M.11.a.1.6. (5) M.2.c.5.7. Ranging 3750 Night retaliation on R.L.	F.16
"	20th		Quiet day.	
"	21st	2 a.m 3.30 a.m	In support of infantry raid - areas M.5.C. were swept with sustained fire. A gun was taken to front line at BOYAU 32 in case of counter attack - this was not required	F.16
	22nd		Generally quiet at all positions. Night firing carried out as per programme. Hostile M.G. showed increased activity during the night.	F.16

Army Form C. 2118.

WAR DIARY
or
INTELLIGENCE SUMMARY
(Erase heading not required.)

Instructions regarding War Diaries and Intelligence Summaries are contained in F.S. Regs., Part II. and the Staff Manual respectively. Title Pages will be prepared in manuscript.

Place	Date	Hour	Summary of Events and Information	Remarks and references to Appendices
MAZINGARBE	23 Ay		Quiet day & night - suspected relief taken place.	O.O. No 15 attached. Marked B.
	24 Aug	7.30am	Relieved by 119 M.G. Co in the LOOS Section.	
		11.30am	Relief complete.	J.H.
NOEUX les MINES	25 "	12 noon	Marched out.	
		3.30 p.m.	Marched to NOEUX les MINES.	J.H.
MARLE les MINES	26 "	11.65am	Arrived MARLE les MINES - billeted.	J.H.
		2 p.m.	Marched out.	
			Arrived BURBURE - billeted.	
BURBURE	27 "		In billets.	J.H.
BURBURE	28	5.30 p.m.	Marched to CHOCQUES.	J.H.
		11 p.m.	Entrained.	
En Route.	29	9.30am	Detrained at HEILLY.	J.H.
		12 noon	Marched to Sandpit MÉAULTE. Arrived 3.30 p.m. Bivouacked.	J.H.
MÉAULTE	30		Bivouacked. Wet day.	
	31.	9.40am	Marched to CITADEL CAMP.	J.H.
		12.5 p.	Arrived CITADEL.	
		4.40 p.	Marched to MONTAUBAN	
		7.20 p.	Arrived MONTAUBAN.	

Army Form C. 2118.

WAR DIARY
or
INTELLIGENCE SUMMARY

(Erase heading not required.)

Place	Date	Hour	Summary of Events and Information	Remarks and references to Appendices
MONTAUBAN	31 Aug	8.15p.m	Relieved 60 M.G. Co. in GUILLEMONT Section. A Sec. took over Rt.R3,R positions 1,2,3,&4. C " " " " 5,6,7,&9. B.D " in reserve.	
"	1st/9/16	3.30am	Relief complete.	

J. Macpire Weaver
Commdg 47 M.G.Co

Secret. 47 M.G. Company.   B Copy No. 7.
          Operation Order No 15.   8th Aug. A16.

1. 47 M.G. Co. will relieve 120 M.G. Co in the LOOS
   Section on the 9th inst.

2. Relief to be complete by 12 noon.

3. A Section will take over R1, R2, R3, R4.
   C   "   "   "   R5, R6, and C1
        D2 (LOOS Defences)
   B   " (LOOS 2 guns) LENS ROAD REDOUBT.
   D   4 and 2 guns 'B' Sec. in reserve.

4. Trench store receipts to be at Coy. H.Q. by 9 a.m.
   10th inst.

5. Coy. H.Q. will open at MAZINGARBE at 12 noon
   9th inst. where completion of relief will be
   notified by wire.

Issued at 6 p.m.
Copy No 1.   A Sec.
 "   " 2   B "
 "   " 3   C "
 "   " 4   D "
 "   " 5   120 M.G. Co.
 "   " 6   Commandant LOOS
 "   " 7   War Diary.
 "   " 8   Filed.

                              [signature]
                              Comd 47 M.G. Coy

Secret.   47 M.G. Company.   A Copy No. 7
          Operation Order No. 16.   23 Aug 1916

1. ● M.G. Co. will be relieved by 119 M.G. Co. in the LOOS Section on night 23/24th inst.

2. 1 Guide per team to be at respective Ration Dumps at 10.30 p.m.

3. All trench stores & reserve S.A.A. to be handed over.

4. The No. 1 of each gun to remain till 10 a.m. 24th inst.

5. Limbers will be at Ration Dumps at 12.30 a.m. After relief sections to return to Coy. H.Q. via LENS ROAD.

6. Trench store receipts to be handed in by 9 a.m. 25th

Issued at 3 p.m.
Copy No 1.   A Sec
  "   " 2   B "
  "   " 3   C "
  "   " 4   D "
  "   " 5   119 M.G.Co
  "   " 6   COMMANDANT LOOS
  "   " 7   War Diary
  "   " 8   Field

J. Hamilton Moore
Commdg. 47 M.G.Co

WAR DIARY.

147th Machine Gun Company

MONTH OF September, 1916.

VOLUME :-

WAR DIARY or INTELLIGENCE SUMMARY

Army Form C. 2118.

(Erase heading not required.)

Place	Date	Hour	Summary of Events and Information	Remarks and references to Appendices
MONTAUBAN	1st Sept		Heavy shelling at intervals, mainly at 4 and 5 positions. Quiet night.	J.M.
"	2nd "		All 2nd line positions shelled at intervals during the day.	J.M.
"	3rd "	8 a.m.	Preparations made for attack	J.M. O.D.No.30 Summary of operations attached. Appendix No.1.
"	4th "		Relieved by 60 M.G. Co. Relief completed at 3.30 a.m. O.O.No.31 attached.	Appendix 1a.
"		6 a.m.	Moved back to CARNOY in Div. Reserve.	J.M.
CARNOY	5th "		Overhauled guns, refilled ammunition and refitted.	J.M.
"	7th "	5.30 p.m.	Took over GUILLEMONT SECTOR. Preparations made for attack on following day.	J.M.
BRIQUETERIE	8th "		TRONES WOOD and GUILLEMONT heavily shelled at intervals O.D. No.32 and summary of Operations attached	Appendix 2, 2a. J.M.
			2 Lieut. L. CHERRY 2 7 O.R. wounded 2 O.R. killed	Remarks on operations attached J.M. sketch map. Appendix 3.
"	9th "	11 p.m.	Relieved by Guards M.G. Co.	J.M. Appendix 4.
"	10th "	2.30 a.m.	Relief complete.	
		6 a.m.	Moved back to CARNOY.	
		2.30 p.m.	Marched to HAPPY VALLEY CAMP.	J.M.
		5 p.m.	Bivouaced.	
HAPPY VALLEY CAMP	11th "	4.25 p.m.	Marched to VAUX sur SOMME.	J.M.
		9 p.m.	Billeted.	

Army Form C. 2118.

WAR DIARY
or
INTELLIGENCE SUMMARY

(Erase heading not required.)

Instructions regarding War Diaries and Intelligence Summaries are contained in F. S. Regs, Part II and the Staff Manual respectively. Title Pages will be prepared in manuscript.

Place	Date	Hour	Summary of Events and Information	Remarks and references to Appendices
VAUX	12th		Refitting	
			Daily programme of overhauling, Drill, and training of reinforcements carried out	T.H
"	17th	1.30pm	Transport marched out for LA CHAUSSÉE	T.H
"	18th	10.15am	Marched out.	
		1pm	Embussed at LA NIVELLE.	
		7pm	Debussed.	
			Marched to VILLERS SUR MARIEUX	T.H
		10pm	Billeted.	
MARIEUX	19th		Resting.	
	20th	7.45am	Marched out.	
		9.4pm	Entrained ABBEVILLE.	T.H
	21st	noon	Left ABBEVILLE	
		9.30am	Arrived BAILLEUL	
		11am	Marched & billeted at METEREN	T.H
METEREN	22nd			
	23rd		Daily programme of training	T.H

249 Wt. W14957/M90 750,000 1/16 J.B.C. & A. Forms/C.2118/12.

Army Form C. 2118.

WAR DIARY
or
INTELLIGENCE SUMMARY

(Erase heading not required.)

Instructions regarding War Diaries and Intelligence Summaries are contained in F. S. Regs., Part II. and the Staff Manual respectively. Title Pages will be prepared in manuscript.

Place	Date	Hour	Summary of Events and Information	Remarks and references to Appendices
	24th	8.45	Marched out to	
		12.30pm	Arrived SCHERPENBERG CAMP. JM	
	25th	11.15am	Inspected by G.O.C. II Army. JM	
	26th		Divl Reserve JM	
	27th	7 p.m	Relieved 48 M.G. Co. in VIERSTRAAT Sector.	O.O. No 33 attached Appendix 5.
			A 2.0 sections in line	
			B.2.0 " in reserve.	
			Relief complete 4.30 p.m	
	28th		Quiet at all positions. JM	
		2.30pm	A few 4.21 dropped in vicinity of BRYNERIE and E.10.7 R.6. No Damage.	
	29th		Night firing carried out on hostile communications O.11a, O.11b, O.19a, O.19.6. JM	
			Very Quiet.	
			Night firing carried out on hostile communications O.11a, O.11b, and WYTSCHAETE - BRICKSTACK Road. JM	
	30th		Quiet Day – not good for observation	
		10h.m	Arr genl Moved by in support of road by Brigade on our right.	
			This was not required.	

1/10/16 –

J. Mayne Major
Commdg 47 Co. M.G.C.

Secret.   47 M.G. Company.   app 1a.   Copy No. 8
          O.O. No 30.   2 September 16
Ref. Sketch 1/10,000

1. The 47th Inf. Bde. will attack GUILLEMONT to-morrow 3rd inst.
   Zero Time will be notified later.

2. For this operation the following attachments will take place.
   (a) A Section (less 1 gun) under 2Lt. WILLIAMSON to 7/LEINSTER REGT.
   (b) C Section (less 2 guns) + 1 gun A Sec. under 2Lt. HADLEY to 8/R. MUNSTER FUSILIERS.
   (c) 2 Guns 'C' Section under 2Lt. BLACKWELL to 6/CONNAUGHT RANGERS.

3. The above officers to report to their respective O.C. Batt'ns before 9 a.m. to-morrow 3rd inst.

4. A carrying party of 3 men per team will be attached from Battalions.

5. 2Lt CHERRY and 3 guns 'B' Section will move up to-night and occupy following positions as local reserve.
   (a) 2 guns in dug-out at JUNCTION OF RAILWAY — M.G. ALLEY. S.24 d. 60.95.
   (b) 1 gun at M.G. HOUSE. S.24 b.7.4.

6. Forward Dumps for ammunition, rations, water and oil will be as follows.
(a) For A Sec. at M.G. House.
(b) For C " at Dug out. S.24.d.60.95.

7. All surplus kits will be left at above Dumps.

8. Further verbal instructions will be given prior to ZERO TIME.

9. Company H.Q. will open at BRIGADE H.Q. 150x N.E. of BERNAFAY WOOD at 11 a.m.

10. 'D' Sec. will remain at MONTAUBAN in reserve.

Issued at 9.15 p.m.
Copy No 1   A Sec.
"   " 2   B "
"   " 3   C "
"   " 4   D "
"   " 5   7/LEINSTER. Ryt.
"   " 6   8/R. MUNSTER Fus.
"   " 7   6/CONNAUGHT Rang.
"   " 8   War Diary
"   " 9   Filed.

G. Hampden Meyer
Comdg 47 A MGC

App. 16.

Secret 47 M.G. Company.   Copy No.
 3 Sept. 1916

O.O. No 31.

1. 47 M.G. Co. will be relieved by 60 M.G. Co. tonight.

2. All belt boxes will be brought back.

3. After relief teams will return independently to Co. H.Q. MONTAUBAN.

Issued at 9.15 p.m.
Copy No 1. A Sec
 " " 2 B "
 " " 3 C "
 " " 4 D "
 " " 5 War Diary
 " " 6 Filed

J. Harper Mayor
Comm'd' 47 Co M.G.C.

Secret   47 M.G. Company.   App 2a   Copy No. 8
                O.O. No 32.   7th Sept. 1916.

1. The 47th Inf. Bde. will take over the GUILLEMONT Sector tonight.

2. For relief and subsequent operations the following attachments will take place
   (a) 'D' Sec.(1en 1 gun) under 2LT SWAFFIELD to 6/R. IRISH Fus. Parade 5.30 p.m.
   (b) 'B' Sec.(1en 1 gun) under 2LT CHERRY to 8/R. MUNSTER Fus. Parade 6.45 p.m.

3. 3 men per team will report to O.C. Section on parade.

4. The remaining teams of B & D Secs. will be available for carry and reinforcements for their respective sections.

5. 1 Gun C Section and 2 guns 'A' Sec. under 2/Lt KENNEDY will stand by in readiness to proceed to the line tomorrow night and act as reserve.
   2/Lt KENNEDY will report at Coy. H.Q. at 8 p.m. 8th inst. for instructions.

6. The forward Dump for ammunition etc will be at ARROW HEAD COPSE.

7. Coy. H.Q. will open at the BRIQUETERIE at 8 p.m. tonight.

Issued at 4 p.m.

Copy No 1. A Sec
 "   " 2   B "
 "   " 3   C "
 "   " 4   D "
 "   " 5   6/R. IRISH Fus.
 "   " 7   8/R. MUNSTER Fus
 "   " 8   War Diary
 "   " 9   FILED.

J. Bompertruya
Comdg 48 MG Co

App. 1.

Operations – 3rd September, 1916

12.20 p.m.	–	7/LEINSTER REGT. reached 1st Objective.
12.24 p.m.	–	"A" Section consolidated.
12.45 p.m.	–	6/CONNAUGHT RANGERS reached 1st Objective.
12.50 p.m.	–	2 Guns "C" Section consolidated.
1.50 p.m.	–	8/R. MUNSTER FUSILIERS report GUILLEMONT captured.
2.30 p.m.	–	3 Guns under 2LT. HADLEY consolidated on SUNKEN ROAD.
5.30 p.m.	–	Owing to failure of 7th DIV. to make good line E. of GINCHY our left was in the air. Ordered 2LT. CHERRY with 2 guns "B" Section up to a position in rear of our left flank covering the gap.
6.25 p.m.	–	2LT. CHERRY reported to be in position. During hostile counter attack on GINCHY and SUNKEN ROAD, the enemy came under concentrated fire from 5 guns at ranges from 600" to 700". Counter attack was beaten off. Rounds fired 5300.
11.0 p.m.	–	Relief by 60 M.G. Coy. commenced.
3.30 a.m.	–	All Sections returned to Coy. H.Q.

Casualties –
    Killed   1 O.R.
    Wounded.   17 O.R.

J. Harper, Major
Cmdg. 47 Coy. M.G.C

App. 2.

Operations – 9th September, 1916.

4.45 p.m. – Attack commenced.

4.50 p.m. – D section advanced supported by 3 guns under 2LT. KENNEDY. The infantry having failed to make good 1st objective gradually fell back on original line. After covering retirement all guns withdrew and consolidated in our old front line.

8.15 p.m. – Report from right flank that strong German counter attack is imminent. Sustained fire was opened by 4 guns for 10 minutes, and maintained at irregular intervals till all was reported quiet. Rounds fired 4300.

11.45 p.m. – Relief by Guards M.G. Coy. commenced.

4.30 p.m. – All sections returned to Coy. H.Q.

Casualties –
    Killed – 1 Officer   2LT. D.C. KENNEDY.
             4 O.R.
    Wounded – 1 Officer   2LT. B. NICHOLLS.
               9 O.R.
    Missing – 1 O.R.

Major
Cmdg. 47 Coy. M.G.C.

App. 3.

Remarks on Operations 3rd and 9th September, 1916.

1. Method of employment of VICKERS guns.

The attachment of M.G. Sections to Battalions for an attack appears to be the method now generally adopted and ensures in my opinion, the best method of co-operation. The O.C. Section, however, should be given a free hand to exercise his powers of initiative — prior to the attack he receives orders from his O.C. Coy. in accordance with the accepted theories — if these are countermanded by O.C. Battalions he is placed in a difficult position.

In my opinion the idea of sending VICKERS guns with the first attacking wave is unsound — if the attack reaches its objective the teams would be able to consolidate with small loss owing to having advanced ahead of the hostile barrage, but this advantage is more than outweighed by the possibility of failure on the part of the infantry to make good their objective — in this case teams would suffer and guns possibly be lost without having had the opportunity to achieve anything.

2. Strength of Teams.

The establishment of a M.G. Coy. is not sufficient to allow of each team to provide its own carrying party. The attachment of men from Battalions just previous to the attack is, I consider, not sound. These men were used by us as ammunition carriers - the time available was too short to teach them thoroughly their job and the signals used - their heart and interest were with their regiments and not with the machine guns. Cases occurred on both occasions of men abandoning their loads to join their battalions, consequently extra work was thrown on to the teams and the smooth working of the ammunition supply interrupted.

3. Supply of Ammunition.

In all cases, 6 belt boxes per gun proved sufficient for the teams to carry over during the first advance to meet the resulting counter-attack. After this had subsided the boxes were refilled from the forward dump.

4. Men should go into action light - leaving all unnecessary kits at forward dump.

5. Rations.

A reserve supply of rations, water, spare barrels and oil should be kept at forward dump.

6. Personnel.

Consider that an addition of 1 Officer, Transport Officer, and 97 O.R., (including 1 cold shoer) is essential.

In active operations each section could find its own carrying party and reinforcements.

In trench warfare each section could arrange the relief of its own teams, thus enabling 16 guns to be in the line continuously.

7 Transport.
- (a) A Transport Officer is essential.
- (b) An extra G.P. Wagon is required - at present the wagon is supposed to carry forage, rations, officers kits and certain articles of store. On the march it was seldom with the company, consequently the officers kits, etc, had to be carried on the limbers - result overloading. In addition, when two days rations are issued the wagon has a full load.
- (c) A M.G. company possesses as many animals as an Infantry Battalion - therefore its establishment of cold shoers ought to be the same.

    It is impossible to expect one man to carry out efficiently the shoeing of 56 animals, especially when on the move.
- (d) A Field Cooker is a matter of necessity. On the march the Company moves invariably as a unit - on two occasions after a tiring day the bivouac was reached in pouring rain, the cooks were not able to keep a fire going in the open, consequently the men were unable to have a hot meal.

    A Field Cooker would prevent many casualties owing to chills, colds, etc., which in its absence, are unavoidable.

Major
Cmdg. 47 Coy. M.G.C.

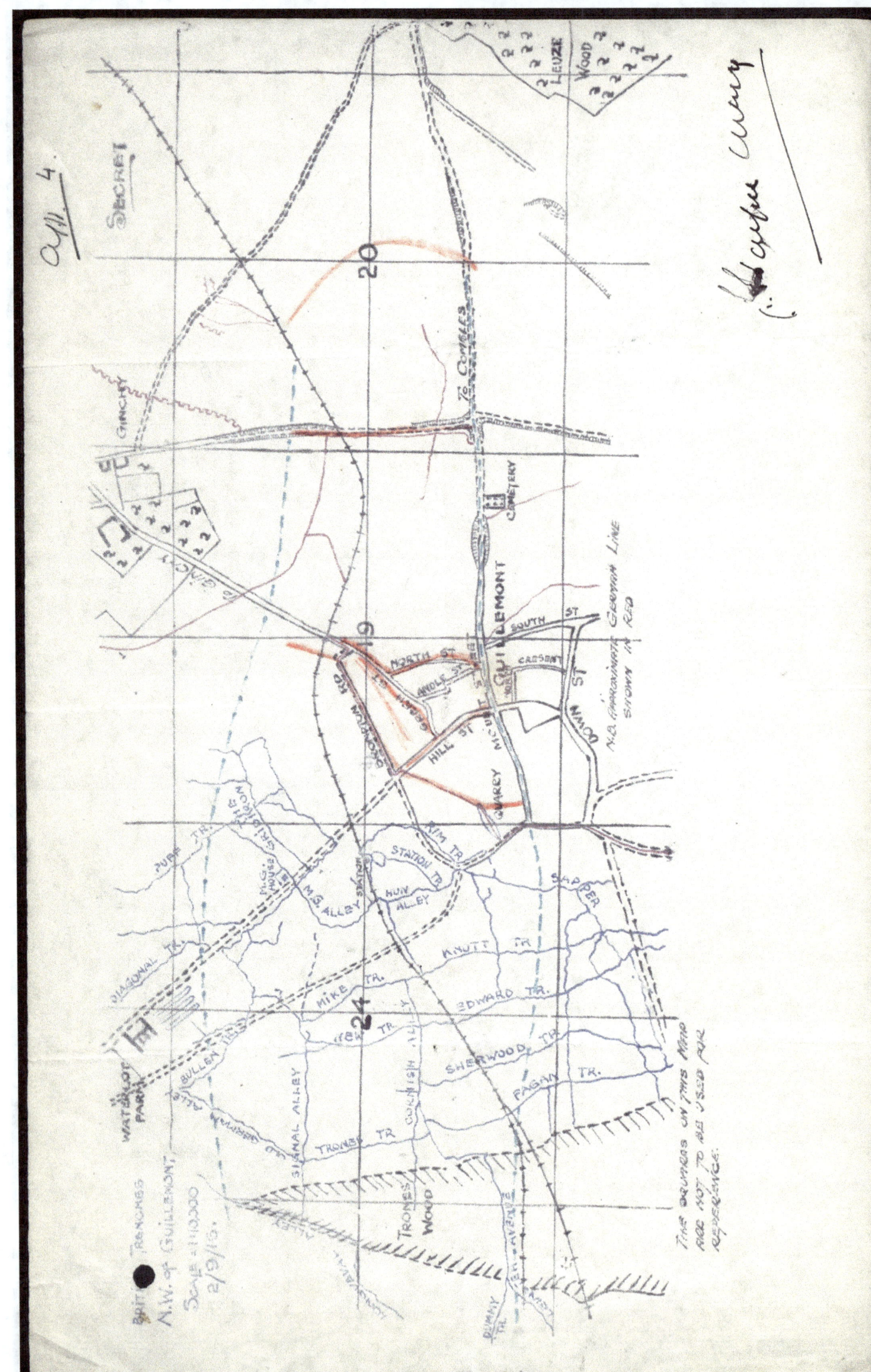

WAR DIARY

MONTH OF OCTOBER, 1916.

VOLUME

47th Machine Gun Company

Army Form C. 2118.

WAR DIARY
or
INTELLIGENCE SUMMARY
(Erase heading not required.)

47th Machine Gun Coy

Place	Date	Hour	Summary of Events and Information	Remarks and references to Appendices
LA CLYTTE	1st Oct		Quiet at all positions. Night firing as usual. J.H.	Ref Sheet 28 S.W.
"	2nd "		Nothing to report by day. During night a hostile M.G. searched our positions at BRYKERIE, but met with no success.	
		7.15 p.m.	Sustained fire opened for 5 minutes on areas O.19.a, O.19.6. Above repeated.	J.H.
		7.40 p.m.		
"	3rd		Very quiet. Intermittent fire carried out during the night on (a) WYTSCHAETE - BRICKSTACH ROAD. (b) SUNKEN ROAD. N.18.6. (c) Area O.7.d.	
"	4th	2 p.m.	D See. relieved C See. at R1, R2, R3, R4. B " A " " R5, R6, & R7. Relief complete 5 p.m.	J.H.
"	5th	"	Quiet at all positions. Hostile M.G. showed slightly increased activity at night on (a) WYTSCHAETE - SUNKEN ROAD. (b) Area O.19.c. Night firing carried out intermittently on	J.H.

2449 Wt. W14957/M90 750,000 1/16 J.B.C. & A. Forms/C.2118/12.

Army Form C. 2118.

WAR DIARY
or
INTELLIGENCE SUMMARY
(Erase heading not required.)

47 MACHINE GUN COY

Map Ref Sheet 28 SW

Place	Date	Hour	Summary of Events and Information	Remarks and references to Appendices
LA CLYTTE	Oct 6th	7 to 8 pm	Quiet at all positions during day. One convoy came from R1 position on area OLGA. Enemy machine gun active around BRYKERIE at night. Intermittent rifle fire from enemy around on areas N16B. O13c. Nothing to report during day.	Chls.
	7th			Chls.
	8th		All quiet during day. Intermittent communication at night on HUTRICS, RED CHATEAU and UNNAMED WOOD	Chls.
	9th		Nothing to report 15 enemy rifle fire on enemy communication or night	Chls.
	10th	2.30pm	Air attack reported near R.S. No damage done. A and C sections relieved B and D front on at night. Relief complete 4.30 pm	Chls.
	11th		Unusual quiet area during day	Chls.
	12th		Some rifle sniping around BRYKERIE during afternoon. Enemy fired on area N16B. O13c. and UNNAMED WOOD	Chls Chateau fire & fight

Army Form C. 2118.

47th MACHINE GUN Coy

MAP REF SHEET 28 SW.

WAR DIARY
or
INTELLIGENCE SUMMARY
(Erase heading not required.)

Place	Date	Hour	Summary of Events and Information	Remarks and references to Appendices
LA CLYTTE	13th		Enemy howitzer reports quiet by day. Intermittent fire carried out at night on:- area N18d, O13c, O15b	
"	14th		Enemy M.G.'s were a little more active than usual. On account of increased activity of enemy working parties on their rear line of communication intermittent fire was kept up all night on following areas: O19A, O19B, O13C.	
"	15th		Enemy M.G's very quiet throughout day and night. C.W. All quiet by day. Fire kept up from 7pm to 1am on road between HOSPICE and RED CHATEAU and on UNNAMED WOOD C.W.	
"	16th 11/46 12.55		TEST GAS ALARM message arrived All ranks at LA CLYTTE fallen in with box respirators at gun Bd All quiet in line. Usual night firing carried out C.W.	a) Working parties on ridge Coy 47th M.G.A Coy

Army Form C. 2118.

WAR DIARY
or
INTELLIGENCE SUMMARY

(Erase heading not required.)

47th MACHINE GUN. Coy
MAP REF. SHEET 28 S.W.

Place	Date	Hour	Summary of Events and Information	Remarks and references to Appendices
LA CLYTTE	Oct 17th		2nd LIEUT E.V. RIDGE and 1 O.R. sent on M.G. Course to CAMIERS. Nothing to report from him. Usual fire carried out at night C/w/	
"	18th		B + D Sections relieved A + C in line. Relief completed at 5 pm. O20C fired on from 8 pm to 10 pm. C/w. Area O20A and O20C.	
"	19th		All quiet in line. Road between HOSPICE and RED CHATEAU fired on during night also area N18B.	
"	to		Fire was maintained throughout the night on following area. RED N18B N18D CHATEAU and road between CHATEAU and HOSPICE. 013C 013A	
"			There was no retaliation. C/w.	

J. Ridley Lieut
for O.C. 47th M.G. Coy

Army Form C. 2118.

47th MACHINE GUN. Coy

MAP REF SHEET 28 SW.

WAR DIARY
or
INTELLIGENCE SUMMARY

(Erase heading not required.)

Instructions regarding War Diaries and Intelligence Summaries are contained in F. S. Regs., Part II. and the Staff Manual respectively. Title Pages will be prepared in manuscript.

Place	Date	Hour	Summary of Events and Information	Remarks and references to Appendices
LA CLYTTE	21st		Nothing to report during day. From 9pm to 10pm usual programme of night firing carried out. C/IC.	
"	22nd		Firing carried out on enemy NIBS, OBC from 7.30 pm to 10.30 pm. Enemy machine gun retaliating on BRYNERIE met with no result. C/IC	
"	23rd		Night firing as usual. C/IC	
"	24th		All quiet in line. Night firing carried out on (a) PLATEAU FARM NIBS (b) RED CHATEAU NIBS (c) Road between RED CHATEAU and HOSPICE (d) UNNAMED WOOD Enemy very active with rifle and machine gun fire during early part of night. MAJOR J.S. HARPER M.C. left to take up appointment as M.G.O. CORPS H.Q. C/IC	J Hyslam Lieut for Major Comm 47th M G Coy

2449 Wt. W14957/M90 750,000 1/16 J.B.C. & A. Forms/C.2118/12.

Army Form C. 2118.

47 MACHINE GUN. COY

REF. SHEET 28 S.W.

WAR DIARY
or
INTELLIGENCE SUMMARY
(Erase heading not required.)

Place	Date	Hour	Summary of Events and Information	Remarks and references to Appendices
LA. CLYTTE	25th		No enemy activity by day. Enemy machine guns busy during early part of night. Rt searched UNNAMED WOOD from 7pm to 10pm. Rt fired at CROSS ROADS in WYTSCHAETE O19D between 7 to 11pm. Rt Traversed road from BRICKSTACK to UNNAMED WOOD from 5.30pm to 10.30pm. Rt fired on PLATEAU FARM N16B and traversed along SUNKEN ROAD N16B to UNNAMED WOOD between from 5.30pm to 10.30pm. Enemy retaliated with M.G. fire on BRYKERIE. A + C Relieved B + D Section. Relief complete 4 pm. C/w.	
"	26th		Nothing to report by day. Night firing was carried out as usual. Target. UNNAMED WOOD Ground between HOSPICE and WYTSCHAETE C/w.	

Army Form C. 2118.

47th MACHINE GUN. Coy

WAR DIARY
or
INTELLIGENCE SUMMARY
(Erase heading not required.)

Place	Date	Hour	Summary of Events and Information	Remarks and references to Appendices
LA CLYTTE	Oct 27th	9pm – 10pm	Indirect fire maintained on (a) SUNKEN ROAD N18B (b) GRAND BOIS O13A (c) CROSS ROADS O20A29	
"	28th		Everything quiet. reported from all fronts.	
		7 – 9pm.	Fire maintained on SUNKEN ROAD, and road between HOSPICE and RED CHATEAU Traversed.	
		10 – 11pm	Above repeated.	
	29th		A demonstration was made on enemy trenches (from line opposite) from N24 A77 to N18 D2S in conjunction with Artillery and French mortars. Six guns fired as follows:	
		5.40 – 5.55 pm	on enemy communication trenches in N24 B and N18 D	
		5.55 – 7.55 pm	on (A) SUNKEN ROAD (B) UNNAMED WOOD (C) Road between RED CHATEAU and BRICKSTACK	
			Few shells fell near R1 and R3 guns. Enemy retaliated and a few shells fell near R1 positions.	

J.W.
Capt
O.C. 47th M.G. Coy

Army Form C. 2118.

WAR DIARY or INTELLIGENCE SUMMARY

(Erase heading not required.)

47th MACHINE GUN. COY

Place	Date Oct.	Hour	Summary of Events and Information	Remarks and references to Appendices
LA CLYTTE	30th		During morning T's gun at BRYKERIE was shelled by by 17cm howitzer. This was repeated during afternoon. Knowing of his gun position thought due to overlooking of R.E. who altered them when altering a dug-out near by. No damage done to matter. Night firing carried on as usual. C.h.	
"	31st	9pm to 11pm	All night harrassing fire ex:- 1 sheet firing behind R6 tracton. Indirect sustained fire carried out on following points (1) Road and Trench 019 B 16 (2) Trench junctions at O13 B 29 (3) Road from N19 S 54 to BRICK STACK 1 Fonquevel C.h.	

Julian Kerr
for Capt Comdg
47th M.G. Coy

WAR DIARY.

FOR

MONTH OF NOVEMBER, 1916.

VOLUME 8

47th Machine Gun Company.

Army Form C. 2118.

47th MACHINE GUN COY
Map Ref Sheet 28 S.W.

WAR DIARY
or
INTELLIGENCE SUMMARY

(Erase heading not required.)

Place	Date 1916	Hour	Summary of Events and Information	Remarks and references to Appendices
LA CLYTTE	Nov 1st	9.20 pm to 10.45	Harass firing carried out throughout the night. Targets engaged i. SUNKEN ROAD } + ground in between. ii. BLACK COT iii. O19.B.16 iv. O13.C.29	
"	Nov 2		VIERSTRAAT was shelled by the enemy between 9.30 A.M and 10.30 A.M on shell falling very near R6 position. Chks. Section Relief afternoon. All quiet throughout day. Indirect fire carried out intermittently between 10.30 – 12.30 pm on following areas O13.c N24.B Chks.	
"	Nov 3		Nothing to report. Harass nightfiring in area N18.d, N18.B, O19.a Chks	

Walter Keir
Lt. O.C. 47th M.G.Coy

Army Form C. 2118.

WAR DIARY
or
INTELLIGENCE SUMMARY

(Erase heading not required.)

47th MACHINE GUN COY
Ref. Sh 21 SW

Place	Date	Hour	Summary of Events and Information	Remarks and references to Appendices
IN CUTTE.	24th		All quiet during day. One M.Gun went active than usual during night in consequence of enemy working parties being observed during the day. The following targets were engaged:-	
		6-11 pm	Hospice 019A73	
		6.30 to 12 mn	Dump 013A49	
		7-1.15 am to 1 am	Red Chateau N16D99	
		7.30 pm to 10.30 pm	Sunken Road N18363	
			There was a little m.g. retaliation. C/W	
	25th		Consolidated fire carried on at night on communication trench at N24B 65.60. 4 guns from 6.30 pm to 11.30 pm C/W	

Chatan Lieut.
to O.C. 47 M.G. Coy

Army Form C. 2118.

WAR DIARY
or
INTELLIGENCE SUMMARY   4-7th MACHINE GUN COY
(Erase heading not required.)

Instructions regarding War Diaries and Intelligence Summaries are contained in F.S. Regs., Part II. and the Staff Manual respectively. Title Pages will be prepared in manuscript.

Place	Date	Hour	Summary of Events and Information	Remarks and references to Appendices
LA CLYTTE	6th		Nothing to report during day. At 10.30 pm 12 guns co-operated with artillery and 4th Inf. Bn in operations shewn in appendix 1 + 2. Total rounds fired 23,250.	Appendix 1 " 2
"		9 a	Capt A. C. SCRIVEN M.C. was killed by a rifle shot. C/s.	
"	7th		There were some hostile shelling on the VIERSTRAAT - KEMMEL ROAD at 8.10 AM. otherwise nothing unusual. Few causies and is right C/s.	
"	8th		Usual fire carried out between 6 pm - 11 pm. Some retaliation by enemy artillery at 7.30 pm on R.T. No damage	
"	9th		Draft of eleven men arrived from BASE. New gun positions near originally VAN KEEP Scotia relied in afternoon. Interdiction fire carried out by R.T., R.B. + R.T. in areas — N 18 B N 16 D O 13 C O 19 A	C/s.

William [signature]
O.C. 47th M.G. Coy.

Army Form C. 2118.

WAR DIARY
or
INTELLIGENCE SUMMARY

47th MACHINE GUN COY

(Erase heading not required.)

Instructions regarding War Diaries and Intelligence Summaries are contained in F. S. Regs., Part II. and the Staff Manual respectively. Title Pages will be prepared in manuscript.

Place	Date Nov.	Hour	Summary of Events and Information	Remarks and references to Appendices
LA CLYTTE	10th		Nothing to report by day. Usual fire carried on at night. Extra M.G.s a little more active than usual during early part of night. CLM.	
"	11th		Over fired mfrom 6.30pm to 12 midnight O15C O16C N18D N18B friendly harrass m/g/fire. Nothing to report. CLM avoid night firing	
	12th		HOSPICE and UNNAMED WOOD fired on during night. SI — VAN KEEP trench mortars fire near about 9.15pm. No damage. CLM	
	14th		Nothing to report by day. Usual indirect fire at night. CLM	

CH Wilson Lt
O/C 47th M.G.Coy

Army Form C. 2118.

WAR DIARY
or
INTELLIGENCE SUMMARY

(Erase heading not required.)

47th MACHINE GUN COY

Instructions regarding War Diaries and Intelligence Summaries are contained in F. S. Regs., Part II. and the Staff Manual respectively. Title Pages will be prepared in manuscript.

Place	Date	Hour	Summary of Events and Information	Remarks and references to Appendices
LA CLYTTE	15th		All quiet both day & night at all guns. Fire carried out as night on areas O13c N18B N18O.	Ohh.
	16th		Capt J. H. Clapham assumed command. Section Relief took place at 2 pm. Today no report from all guns both day & night. More indirect & sustained fire than usual was carried out from 11pm – 10pm, that interval being the night. Guns fired on. O13c O15a O13b N18b Clb	Ohh.
"	17th		Fire was carried out on same areas as 15 & 16th. Intermittent fire was carrying out at night on DUMP at O13d73	Ohh.
"	18th		All guns report "all quiet". Usual fire carried out.	Ohh.

Clapham Lt
for 47 M.G.Coy

2449 Wt. W14957/Mgo 750,000 1/16 J.B.C. & A. Forms/C.2118/12.

Army Form C. 2118.

WAR DIARY
or
INTELLIGENCE SUMMARY
(Erase heading not required.)

Ref. Sht 28 SW.

Place	Date	Hour	Summary of Events and Information	Remarks and references to Appendices
LA CLYTTE	19/5		No desert of enemy to report. Shared fire carried on as usual between 6.30 p to midnight. O/N	
	20	6.30p 8p	All gun fires during the night as follows:— R5 R6 on Targets at 013c 15 N18B 83 R7 K18D 013c 73 There was no retaliation.	
			R1 R3 R4 } fired intermittently throughout the night on { 013c91 019a17 N18D71 019a90 O/N	
	21/5		Nothing to report from the line. Shared fire carried out at night of enemy area. Cpy H.Q. and ammn station moved at 2.30 pm during afternoon and renewed by 11th Field Ambulance at SCHERRENBERG to their vacated CHW	

A Watson Lieut
for O.C. 11th H.O. Coy

WAR DIARY or INTELLIGENCE SUMMARY

Army Form C. 2118.

Ref Shu 28 S.W.

Place	Date Nov	Hour	Summary of Events and Information	Remarks and references to Appendices
SCHERPENBERG	22nd		Nothing to report by day. Intermittent fire carried out during night by 2 guns. Nil.	
"	23rd		All quiet reported from our guns during day. Night firing on HOSPICE, SUNKEN ROAD carried out from 6.30pm to 11 pm. Strong O.P. returned to BASE indifferent. Section relief carried out at 9 A.M. O.W.	
"	24th		Our guns report normal quietness by day. Harassing fire was carried out. HOSPICE to SUNKEN Rd } throughout the night and ground in between } Ball WYTSCHAETE } from 7pm to 1 am. UNNAMED WOOD N.16.D.10.13 from 6.15-11pm Enemy trench standard mortars were active on YAN KEEP terrain M _'ein were seen to fire on the VIERSTRAAT Road from 6.30pm to 11pm. O.W. O.W. Wilson Lt OC 47 Bty Bn	

Army Form C. 2118.

WAR DIARY
or
INTELLIGENCE SUMMARY
(Erase heading not required.)

Ref Sheet 28 SW

Place	Date	Hour	Summary of Events and Information	Remarks and references to Appendices
SCHERPENBERG	25th		Nothing to report by day. Our own guns were very active, firing few rounds from 7 pm to 11 pm on the following targets — HOSPICE, BRICKSTACK, Ground between the HOSPICE and UNNAMED WOOD, BLACK COT, UNNAMED WOOD and the C.T. in it, RED CHATEAU and along the SUNKEN ROAD. A hostile M.G. was seen firing from the BLACK COT, & was engaged by one of ours, and successfully put out of action with H.E. shrapnel at 8.30 pm.	
	26th		R6 & R7 were shelled with H.E. during the night, no damage was done. Usual night firing was carried out throughout the night. There seem no retaliation.	

J. Wilson Lieut
for O.C. 14th N.Z. Coy

Army Form C. 2118.

WAR DIARY
or
INTELLIGENCE SUMMARY.
(Erase heading not required.)

Ref Sheet 28.S.W.

Place	Date	Hour	Summary of Events and Information	Remarks and references to Appendices
SCHERPENBERG	Nov 27th		Nothing to report by day. Intermittent fire carried out as usual from 5.30pm to 12 midnight, and on O13.c, BRICKSTACK, BLACK COT & HOSPICE were fired on to 3 a.m. chts	
"	28th		The following areas were fired on throughout the night:- O13.c N.18.d O19.a N.16.d Enemy m.gs were also active up to midnight. chts	
"	29th		All quiet efforts by all guns by day. On account of sharp frost all guns fired at intervals throughout the night, at the following layoffs. Communication Trench N16D 83 O19A19 to O19A6.10 " N18D98 UNNAMED WOOD	

J Wilson
Lt
O.C. 87th M.G. Coy

Army Form C. 2118.

WAR DIARY
or
INTELLIGENCE SUMMARY.
(Erase heading not required.)

Instructions regarding War Diaries and Intelligence Summaries are contained in F.S. Regs., Part II. and the Staff Manual respectively. Title pages will be prepared in manuscript.

Place	Date	Hour	Summary of Events and Information	Remarks and references to Appendices

SCHERPENBERG	Nov 24th		SUNKEN ROAD
			 RED CHATEAU
			 HOSPICE
			 Coy by day awaited gun teams to carry on work on position etc by 1 day.
			 The following joined from BASE DEPOT
			    2nd Lt B.J. PHILLIPS posted to A Section
			    2nd Lt S.H. BURNS posted to D Section
			    1 O.R.	

	25th		All quiet reports from all guns during day Our night defensive fire were carried out all night on i HOSPICE and Communication trench O19A88 ii BLACK COT " O13c03 iii RED CHATEAU " N18B82 iv Trenches at O13c99	

Army Form C. 2118.

WAR DIARY
or
INTELLIGENCE SUMMARY.
(Erase heading not required.)

Instructions regarding War Diaries and Intelligence Summaries are contained in F.S. Regs., Part II. and the Staff Manual respectively. Title pages will be prepared in manuscript.

Place	Date	Hour	Summary of Events and Information	Remarks and references to Appendices
	Nov.			
SCHERPENBERG	30		(x) Trenches and Front line. O13 c 38	
			Enemy machine guns retaliated strongly.	

Secret. 47 M.G. Company.   Copy No 6.
         Operation Order No 33.

1. 47 Co. will take over the VIERSTRAAT sector for 47 M.G. Co. this afternoon 27th inst.

2. A and C Sections will parade at 2 p.m. and march to BASIEGE Farm. Route LA CLYTTE — X Roads KEMMEL CHURCH — BASIEGE Farm where guides will meet.

3. A Sec. will take over left sector.
   C "   "   "   "   right sector.

4. B and D Sec. will parade at 4.30 p.m. and move to Tented Camp M.G.d.

5. Coy. H.Q will open at M.G.d. at 6 p.m.

Issued at 12 noon.
Copy No 1. A Sec.
  "   " 2. B Sec.
  "   " 3. C Sec.
  "   " 4. D Sec.
  "   " 5. 48 M.G. Co.
  "   " 6. War Diary
  "   " 7. Filed.

Comdg. 47 M.G. Co

WAR DIARY FOR MONTH OF DECEMBER, 1916.

VOLUME 9

47th Machine Gun Company.

Army Form C. 2118.

WAR DIARY
or
INTELLIGENCE SUMMARY.
(Erase heading not required.)

Place	Date	Hour	Summary of Events and Information	Remarks and references to Appendices
SCHERPENBERG	1st		All quiet reported from line by day. Our guns very active throughout night firing 8250 rounds on HOSPICE + C.Ts O19A88; BLACK COT and trenches N18D02; BRICKSTACK trench O13C70 to O13C75; UNNAMED WOOD; Enemy M.G.s retaliated & searched for guns but were being engaged by our M.G's. secured fire. All quiet throughout night. Sick - NIL. Strength of Coy offs 10 OR 164. O/WS	
do	2nd		Nothing to report by day. Raid was carried out by Brigade on our left which it Coy co-operated. Line was opened at 5pm in the following details:- N18D43 to N18D48 N18B45 to N18D35 - N18D76 SUNKEN ROAD + trench Communication trench vertically O13C70 to O13C75 reached at N18D3 UNNAMED WOOD Total rounds fired 16,500. Throughout night enemy guns searched for our positions unsuccessfully. Sick evacuated 1OR. O/WS	O/Wilson Lt Col 9th Highrs

T2134. Wt. W708-776. 500000. 4/15. Sir J.C. & S.

Army Form C. 2118.

WAR DIARY
or
INTELLIGENCE SUMMARY
(Erase heading not required.)

Instructions regarding War Diaries and Intelligence Summaries are contained in F.S. Regs., Part II. and the Staff Manual respectively. Title pages will be prepared in manuscript.

Place	Date	Hour	Summary of Events and Information	Remarks and references to Appendices
SCHERPENBERG	Dec 3rd		There was some hostile shelling in the vicinity of R6 - R7 during day. No damage. Manual wire for carried out at night. CWS	
do	4		Bomber relief took place. A.C Section relieved 109th Coy, M.G.C in SPANBROEK SECTOR (N 30 c). Seven position taken over - 15pm kept in reserve at FRENCHMAN'S FARM (N 34 B. Relief of this sector commenced at 2.30pm & completed at 7.15 and 9pm. S4, R1, R3, R4, R5 positions taken over & relieved by 48th M.G Coy. Relief complete 10.30 AM. R6 & R7 positions relieved by 124th Coy. Relief commenced 9.30 AM and completed 10.50 PM. All reliefs carried out without mishap.	
		10.30pm	Our relief correct reported Bugaclo 9.35pm. No 7663 Pte CROWLEY M.J tried by F.G.C.M. CWS	

signature

Army Form C. 2118.

Instructions regarding War Diaries and Intelligence
Summaries are contained in F.S. Regs., Part II.
and the Staff Manual respectively. Title pages
will be prepared in manuscript.

WAR DIARY
or
INTELLIGENCE SUMMARY.
(Erase heading not required.)

Place	Date	Hour	Summary of Events and Information	Remarks and references to Appendices
SCHERPENBERG	Dec 5		Nothing to report from line. Relieved fire was carried out throughout night on following targets. KRUISSTRAAT CROSS ROADS N30d77 O25c51 N36 B3 On account of very severe frost all guns had permanently thawing out night. Work was carried on throughout our night improving dug-outs and emplacements. Sick evacuated 1 O.R. C.W.S.	
do.	6th		Heavy trench mortaring near No 3 gun in front line reported. Also enemy M.G. fire on roads around FRENCHMANS FARM. Targets fired on :- N30 D64 : O31 A04 : N30 d38 No casualties. There was a little western retaliation. O25 a81 : O31 A08 : C.W. Reinforcements :- 1 O.R. Movement due to system.	

T2134. Wt. W708—776. 500000. 4/15. Sir J. C. & S.

Army Form C. 2118.

WAR DIARY
or
INTELLIGENCE SUMMARY.
(Erase heading not required.)

Place	Date	Hour	Summary of Events and Information	Remarks and references to Appendices
SCHERPENBERG	7th		Fairly quiet reported from line. Heard intense fire carried out at night in area O.25.c. N.30.A. N.30.D. Hostile M.G. emplacements & dugouts catching on. Sick evac. 1 O.R.	
	8th		Strength of Coy. 10 Off. 164 O.R. Indirect fire in area N.30.A : N.30.D : N.36.B : O.25.c : carried out.	
	9th		Hostile M.G.s retaliated in No 1 Gun without effect. Chs. Nothing to report except increased enemy lights. He actively aright. Indirect fire as indicated. Chs.	
	10th		No events of importance to record.	
	11th	9.30 AM	Concentrated indirect fire carried out on enemy Cels B - D section left. HQ to take over from D.C. Section in batln. Relief reported carried at 11.30 AM. Garrison area from N.30.A. N.30.D. O.25.C. N.30.B. Chs. Reinforcement 5 O.R. (drivers)	

[signature]

Army Form C. 2118.

WAR DIARY
or
INTELLIGENCE SUMMARY.
(Erase heading not required.)

Instructions regarding War Diaries and Intelligence Summaries are contained in F.S. Regs., Part II. and the Staff Manual respectively. Title pages will be prepared in manuscript.

Place	Date	Hour	Summary of Events and Information	Remarks and references to Appendices
SCHAFENBERG	Dec 12th		Shelling by SP6 and SP6 reported from trenches. Sustained and concentrated. Casualties:— Reinforcements from BASE:— 9 OR 1 OR (wounded). ChB Departures:— Same as casual carried out. ChB	
	13th		Nothing to report.	
do	14th		French mortar activity around front line from upmost from trenches. Fire carried on at night in area N 30 D N 36 B N 30 C N 30 A. Troops in trenches dug-outs and emplacements arrived in. ChB	Chhalen hurr or up piecer

T.2134. Wt. W708—776. 500000. 4/15. Sir J.C. & S.

Army Form C. 2118.

WAR DIARY
or
INTELLIGENCE SUMMARY.
(Erase heading not required.)

Instructions regarding War Diaries and Intelligence Summaries are contained in F. S. Regs., Part II. and the Staff Manual respectively. Title pages will be prepared in manuscript.

Place	Date	Hour	Summary of Events and Information	Remarks and references to Appendices
Schuytershoef	15th		Trench mortar activity reported. Fire carried out during night on cross road and communication trenches in area N30D, N36B, N30C, N30A. Nos 3 & 4 guns fired at intervals on enemy front & support line trenches.	
	16		Strength of Coy 10 offrs. 199 OR. Nothing to report from line. Night firing as usual carried out. Casualties. 1 OR sent sick.	
	17		Enemy seemed very nervous throughout day and night. Burin night concentrated & sustained fire of 3 guns was carried out on area N36B. Area N30D, N30A were also fired on.	

O.C. of [signature]

Army Form C. 2118.

Instructions regarding War Diaries and Intelligence Summaries are contained in F.S. Regs., Part II. and the Staff Manual respectively. Title pages will be prepared in manuscript.

WAR DIARY
or
INTELLIGENCE SUMMARY.
(Erase heading not required.)

Place	Date	Hour	Summary of Events and Information	Remarks and references to Appendices
SCHEARPENBERG	Dec 18th		Some artillery activity during day. Relief of B & D sections by A & C sections carried out. Completion of relief reported at 11:20 A.M. Area N 36 B. O/5 & C fired on Enemy front & support line occasionally. However throughout night. Casualties. Arrivals 2 O.R. from BASE. Chls.	
"	19		Nothing to Report. Usual fire carried on at night. Chls	
"	20		Nothing to Report. Usual targets fired on throughout night. Casualties. 3 O.R. Details at 6:30 A.M. in transit to BASE. Chls	
"	21	7:50 AM	HEAVY BRANCH M.G.C. fire was opened over Transport lines & was returned by 8:10 PM. A decrease in enemy M.G. activity is noticeable. Indirect fire as usual carried out at night by day, but some shelling near No. 2 gun at night. Chls	
			Chilwood to octogrphic	

T./134. Wt. W708—776. 500000. 4/15. Sir J.C. & S.

Army Form C. 2118.

WAR DIARY
or
INTELLIGENCE SUMMARY.
(Erase heading not required.)

Instructions regarding War Diaries and Intelligence Summaries are contained in F. S. Regs., Part II. and the Staff Manual respectively. Title pages will be prepared in manuscript.

Place	Date	Hour	Summary of Events and Information	Remarks and references to Appendices
SCHERPENBERG	Dec 21st		Trench mortars active during day. Aircraft over O25A, N36B, N30D were fired on, and the enemy parapet traversed by No.3 gun. Strength of Coy. 16 off. 148 O.R.	
do	22nd		A little artillery and trench mortar activity around No.3 gun. On account of infantry patrols very little indirect fire could be carried out. Casualties. NOR. O.R. Heavies, M.G.C. at 6.40 A.M. The following areas were fired on last night. N36B O31A N30D	
do	23rd		Nothing to report.	

WAR DIARY
or
INTELLIGENCE SUMMARY.
(Erase heading not required.)

Army Form C. 2118.

Place	Date	Hour	Summary of Events and Information	Remarks and references to Appendices
SCHERPENBERG	25		"Everything quiet" reported from lines. A little indirect fire was carried out on area N31A. Casualties. Arrived Two from 24th Div. G. Coy. Chls.	
"	26th		Activity of artillery, trench mortars + m.g. above normal. 30 shells of small calibre fell near No 1 gun near FRENCHMANS FARM between 5 + 6 p.m. doing no damage. Relief of A+C Sections carried out. Relief complete 11.45A.M. Sustained indirect fire carried out on area O31A. N30D. N36B N36D. Chls	
do	27		Line reported normal. Firing as usual carried out. Casualties. Arrivals 6 O.R. (5 Drivers 1 Armourer). Chls	

J Nelson Lt
24/4/1916

WAR DIARY or INTELLIGENCE SUMMARY

Army Form C. 2118.

Place	Date	Hour	Summary of Events and Information	Remarks and references to Appendices
SCHERPENBERG	1916 Sep 28th		Shared artillery + trench-mortar activity reported. Indirect fire was carried on throughout the night on Communication Trenches + Crossroads behind enemy lines. During the night much work was done on enemy trenches, dug-outs. ChK. Strength of Coy 10 off 161 o.r.	
	29th		Much rain during the last 24 hours, and dugouts uninhabitable. Front line generally excessively muddy from his front line. Our guns showed increased activity at night. Work on trenches carried on ChK	
do	30th		Enemy artillery active throughout day, chiefly with shrapnel. 4,500 rounds S.A.A. were fired in air by 5 guns on Freezing Strong Point +CT. 025 B08 X R.a. + C.T. N36A38 R.a. + C.T. N30D77 No 3 gun withdrawn to S.P.6 at 9.30 pm. Enemy M.G.s also active throughout night. ChK	N36 628 031 A 05 w OKolaark z47 rr 60

T.J.134. Wt. W.708—776. 500000. 4/15. Sir J. C. & S.

Army Form C. 2118.

WAR DIARY
or
INTELLIGENCE SUMMARY.
(Erase heading not required.)

Place	Date	Hour	Summary of Events and Information	Remarks and references to Appendices
SCHERPENBERG	31st	RCE	Rather of importance to report from line except usual slight trench-mortar activity. Guns fired throughout the night on areas N 30 D 87 O 25 B 08 N 30 D 77 N 36 B There was a little m.g. retaliation. No casualties.	

C Watson Lieut
Wyverner

WAR DIARY for month of JANUARY, 1917.

VOLUME 10

47th Machine Gun Company.

Vol 9

Army Form C. 2118.

WAR DIARY
or
INTELLIGENCE SUMMARY.
(Erase heading not required.)

Ref. Sheet 28 S.H.

Instructions regarding War Diaries and Intelligence Summaries are contained in F.S. Regs., Part II. and the Staff Manual respectively. Title pages will be prepared in manuscript.

Place	Date	Hour	Summary of Events and Information	Remarks and references to Appendices
SCHERPENBERG	1st 16/1/17	10.30am	SP6 received some attention from enemy's artillery one shell safely damaging gun position. Another gun was dug out. M4 gun also shelled. Remainder of day comparatively quiet. Artillery activity on both sides has shown a decided increase. Casualties 1 O.R. wounded from 1st R. MUNSTER Fus. Indirect fire was carried on at night on areas N30 D8⟩ O25 B ⟩ N30 D77 ⟩ O25 A ⟩	
		1pm	An enemy search light was also engaged which was immediately extinguished. There were the names unavoidably not included 2/Lt C.H. ENTWISLE and 2.O.R. proceeded on leave to U.K.	

(signatures)

Army Form C. 2118.

WAR DIARY
or
INTELLIGENCE SUMMARY.
(Erase heading not required.)

Instructions regarding War Diaries and Intelligence Summaries are contained in F. S. Regs., Part II. and the Staff Manual respectively. Title pages will be prepared in manuscript.

Place	Date	Hour	Summary of Events and Information	Remarks and references to Appendices
SCHERPENBERG	1919 Jan. 2nd	8.30am	Captn J. H. CLAPHAM returned from leave to U.K.	
		9.15	A.C Section guns returned from overhaul by Divisional Armourers Shop. All quiet during day reported from line. Guns fired throughout the night on roads and communication trenches at N 36 B 38 N 30 D 77 O 25 D 77 Ammunition, stores, water carried in on night from emplacement. Divising further material supplies etc at N°1, N°2, N°4 + N°6 positions. ChC	
do	3rd	9.15am	Section relief carried out. A.C. relieving D + B sections respectively + taking over positions 1, 2, 5, SP8, and 3, 4, 6, 7 respectively. Relief reported complete 12.35 pm.	

WAR DIARY
or
INTELLIGENCE SUMMARY.
(Erase heading not required.)

Army Form C. 2118.

Place	Date	Hour	Summary of Events and Information	Remarks and references to Appendices
SCHERPENBERG	3rd (continued)	10.5pm	"TEST S.O.S" signal received from Brigade.	
		10.15	B.D. sedan ready to move off.	
		11.6pm	Transport & sedans moved off. Returning at 11.15pm.	
		10.45pm	TEST S.O.S. received by Advanced H.Q. H.Q. turns immediately laid to barrage fire according to Orr Defence Scheme.	
		11.30pm	"SITUATION NORMAL" received. Indirect fire in usual carried on throughout night. Increased artillery activity reported from line. Indirect fire in area Rds and C.T. arrived on throughout night.	
			N 30 B	
			N 30 D	
			O 26 D	
			O 19 C	
Croualtu.	4th		1 O.R. evac. Sick. 2 O.R. to Base for transfer to Home Establishment.	Ypres[?] infantry[?]

Army Form C. 2118.

WAR DIARY
or
INTELLIGENCE SUMMARY.
(Erase heading not required.)

Place	Date	Hour	Summary of Events and Information	Remarks and references to Appendices
SCHERPENBERG	Jan 5th		Activity, both of artillery and trench mortars, above normal reported from line. Enemy night fire on following areas was carried out	
			N 30 B	
			O 31 F A	
			O 25 C	
			N 30 D	
			Work was carried out on drainage of Kemmel, building of dug-outs, emplacements etc.	
			Strength of Coy - 10 offrs 177 OR Chh.	
	do	6th	Usual activity by day. Usual fire carried on throughout night on enemy C.T.s etc. Nothing to report. c/h	

Chapman Lieut
for O.C. 171 Coy
R.E.

Army Form C. 2118.

WAR DIARY
or
INTELLIGENCE SUMMARY.
(Erase heading not required.)

Instructions regarding War Diaries and Intelligence Summaries are contained in F.S. Regs., Part II. and the Staff Manual respectively. Title pages will be prepared in manuscript.

Place	Date	Hour	Summary of Events and Information	Remarks and references to Appendices
SCHERPENBERG	Jan 7th		Artillery activity above normal both day and night. All firm in line 'stood-to' during heavy bombardment on our immediate right between 3.30 pm & 5 pm. Indirect fire carried out throughout night on usual targets by guns Nos 1, 5, 6 and 7. Casualties - Nil. 2nd Lt E.E.L. WHITEHEAD and 1 O.R. proceeded on leave to U.K.	OK
	8th		Artillery fire normal at periods throughout the day, in consequence of which, on BRIGADE instructions No 7 gun was moved up to SHELL FARM (N36c) at dusk. Fire by Nos 1, 5 & 6 guns was directed on enemy communication trenches, roads and strong-points, fire being maintained all night. Work on shaft was carried on during night.	OK

O.W.Walsh Lieut
for O.C. 47th M.G.Coy

WAR DIARY
INTELLIGENCE SUMMARY

Army Form C. 2118.

Place	Date	Hour	Summary of Events and Information	Remarks and references to Appendices
SCHERPENBERG	Jan 9th		Intermittent shelling by both sides throughout day, one shell striking the side of dugout at No 3 Position but doing slight damage. Firing on usual scale carried on throughout night, but exception of some retaliation by enemy M.G. on NoB from there is nothing to report. Took un usual stand to night. Casualties Nil.	
	10th 9.15am		Section relief took place. B Section relieving A section in Positions 1, 2, 5 - SP8 D " " " " 3, 4, 6, 7 C " " " " Relief was hampered owing Casualty: 1 O.R. wounded. during DAYLIGHT CORNER. Sustained Indirect fire when transport reefs on evenin- O 13 A O 25 A Work on emplacements, dugouts etc carried on	9/1/

Army Form C. 2118.

WAR DIARY
or
INTELLIGENCE SUMMARY
(Erase heading not required.)

Ref Sheet 28 SW

Place	Date	Hour	Summary of Events and Information	Remarks and references to Appendices
SCHAAPENBERG	Jan 11th		Artillery and trench mortar activity normal. Nothing to report from line by day. 3 O.R. proceeded on leave to U.K.	OC
	12th		Considerable increase in enemy artillery and trench mortar activity. No damage done to positions in line. Sustained fire on unusual targets carried out through out the night. Casualties 1 O.R. evacuated sick. Total strength 16 off. 182 O.R.	OC
	13th		Persistent rain causing trenches to collapse. A few heavy shells fell during the morning near one or two guns in line but doing no material damage. Fire as usual throughout night. Casualties — 3 O.R. evacuated sick.	OC

J Holden Lieut
4/5 7 MGC

Army Form C. 2118.

WAR DIARY
or
INTELLIGENCE SUMMARY.
(Erase heading not required.)

Instructions regarding War Diaries and Intelligence Summaries are contained in F.S. Regs., Part II. and the Staff Manual respectively. Title pages will be prepared in manuscript.

Place	Date	Hour	Summary of Events and Information	Remarks and references to Appendices
SCHERPENBERG	JAN 14th		Severe frosts rendering carrying of guns difficult.	
do	15th		Normal. Reported frostbites in the line. O.R.W.	
			Summary of events between these dates.	
			Activity of all branches of enemy artillery and trench mortars noticeable.	
			Indirect fire on usual targets has been carried on every night — no unusual	
			Relief of Sections in line	
	17th		A Sect. relieved D Sect.	
			C " B "	
	24th		R " A "	
			D " C "	
			Strength of Bn.	
	19th		10 Offrs. 170 O.R.	
	26th		10 Offrs. 171 O.R.	
			Casualties. 15th. 3 O.R. accidentally wounded through bomb	

Army Form C. 2118.

WAR DIARY
or
INTELLIGENCE SUMMARY.
(Erase heading not required.)

Place	Date	Hour	Summary of Events and Information	Remarks and references to Appendices
SCHERPENBURG			exploding near	
	21st		1 O.R. wounded through accidental discharge of revolver.	
			Inter Coy Transfer.	
			Sergt NEBSTER A.E. to 164 Coy as C.Q.M.S. Y.W.	
	3rd			

C Wilson Lieut
for O/C
47th M.G. Co

WAR DIARY.

FOR MONTH OF FEBRUARY, 1917.

VOLUME 11

UNIT:- 47th Machine Gun Company

Army Form C. 2118.

WAR DIARY
or
INTELLIGENCE SUMMARY.
(Erase heading not required.)

Place	Date	Hour	Summary of Events and Information	Remarks and references to Appendices
SCHAAPENBURG	Feb 1st		Between 5am & 6.30am the enemy heavily bombarded our line with artillery of large calibre, being their first all gun strafe "alight-to". In spite of one direct hit at No 2 boiler there were no casualties. The remainder of the day passed comparatively quietly except for a bombardment lasting 5 minutes at 4pm. This was carried out as follows shrapnel the right No 6 } fired on H.E. flyp. hood and C.T.s to northwards No 5 } at N30 D. Total rounds fired 3,000. Casualties Arundo 1 O.R. from C.C.S. Ypres Nil	

[signature]

WAR DIARY or INTELLIGENCE SUMMARY

Army Form C. 2118.

Place	Date	Hour	Summary of Events and Information	Remarks and references to Appendices
SCHERPENBERG	2nd Feb		All quiet reported from line. At 11AM No 2 gun opened fire on enemy aircraft during night. No 1 gun fired on LENFER WOOD No 5 " " CROSS ROADS N30D No 6 " " C.T. at N30009 C.T. at 015D22 No 7 " " Total rounds fired 3/50. All damage done by enemy bombardment of the town repaired during night. Coy strength 10 offrs 171 O.R. O.W.W.	
do	3rd		Enemy very quiet reported from line. There was great aerial activity throughout the morning, but all enemy planes were beyond range of our M Guns. Fire was carried out on LENFER WOOD; Strong Points N30D88 / CROSS ROADS N30D X Roads 03A44 O.W.W.	
do	4th		Casualties: 2 O.R. joined from BASE DEPOT.	
			During morning Coy H.Q. were transferred to BEEHIVE DUGOUTS	

[signature]

Army Form C. 2118.

WAR DIARY
or
INTELLIGENCE SUMMARY.
(Erase heading not required.)

Instructions regarding War Diaries and Intelligence Summaries are contained in F.S. Regs., Part II. and the Staff Manual respectively. Title pages will be prepared in manuscript.

Place	Date	Hour	Summary of Events and Information	Remarks and references to Appendices
SCHERPENBERG	4th (cont'd)		All quiet reports from guns positions on line. Sustained indirect fire on enemy C.T's, strong points and line of approach maintained as routine throughout night. The supply of rations has for the last three days been very short.	
			Owing to lack of fuel and the mens frozen great difficulty is being experienced in the line in keeping the guns ready for instant action.	
			At 9.30 AM the two sections on the line (A+C) were reinforced by B sect.	
	5th		All quiet reported from line with exception of some harrassing of our trenches and strong points between 2.30 + 4 pm. Fire as usual was carried out throughout the night on Chandelier Nr. N 36 b 99, N 30 d 98, N 30 D 88. etc.	Observation 4 to 5th Nov 00

Army Form C. 2118.

WAR DIARY
or
INTELLIGENCE SUMMARY.
(Erase heading not required.)

Instructions regarding War Diaries and Intelligence Summaries are contained in F.S. Regs., Part II. and the Staff Manual respectively. Title pages will be prepared in manuscript.

Place	Date	Hour	Summary of Events and Information	Remarks and references to Appendices
SCHERPENBERG	Feb 6		All quiet reports from teams in line. Indirect & sustained fire on following targets maintained throughout night.	
			N30 D 56·32 N30 C 66 90 L'ENFER WOOD and C.T.s to NORTHWARDS	
			Total rounds fired 4,000.	
			Casualties 1 O.R.	
	7th		Nothing to report from line. Inter-section relief started 9.15 A.M. A Sect. arrived in trench 2.30 pm. Firing as usual carried out throughout night, mostly with no retaliation except for enemy M.G. fire on N° 7 gun.	
			Casualties Nil. Owing to enlivenment officers fear no - or very little work can be done in the	club
	8th		All quiet by day. Enemy evening heavy artillery strafe on immediate left and right of Sector. Usual firing carried on at night.	
			Casualties. Nil.	CW

Chandler/Lieut
for O.C. 7 M.G. Coy.

Army Form C. 2118.

WAR DIARY
or
INTELLIGENCE SUMMARY.
(Erase heading not required.)

Place	Date	Hour	Summary of Events and Information	Remarks and references to Appendices
SOMERPEN CURS	9th		There was some artillery liveliness reported during the morning. Otherwise situation quiet. Throughout the night guns fired on Roads, cross roads, communication trenches and works in N36B3 N30D 02SD 02SC 02SB H.250. No of rounds expended throughout night on "Barrage nats", clearing loopholes etc. was carried on BB217 10ft 175 OR. Strength of Coy reported as 111th TA. Casualties.	
		11am	1 Officer and 1 O.R. from BASE DEPOT. 2nd Lieut G.W.H. MERRY taken on strength of Coy as supernumerary. 1 O.R. evacuated sick to 111th FA.	CWS

C Watson Lieut
for OC 47th MG Coy

Army Form C. 2118.

WAR DIARY
or
INTELLIGENCE SUMMARY.
(Erase heading not required.)

Instructions regarding War Diaries and Intelligence Summaries are contained in F.S. Regs., Part II. and the Staff Manual respectively. Title pages will be prepared in manuscript.

Place	Date	Hour	Summary of Events and Information	Remarks and references to Appendices
SCHERPENBERG	Feb 10th		Nothing to report during the normal transport night. Casualties.	
	11th		1 OR joined from Advd. Horse Dept. A little shelling of front line during afternoon reported from him. Otherwise nothing to report. Thing as usual carried out. Anti-aircraft positions improved during night. Casualties Nil.	
	12th		Nothing to report from him. Sustained fire carried out throughout night on following areas. O15D O31A N30D N31A O25D	
	13th		One quiet reported by day. Indirect fire was carried out as follows on areas.	
	12 N to 4 pm		N30D O31A O25D No. of rounds fired 250. 1 OR from BASE DEPOT.	

C/ Nelson Lt
4/7th Middx

WAR DIARY
or
INTELLIGENCE SUMMARY.
(Erase heading not required.)

Army Form C. 2118.

Instructions regarding War Diaries and Intelligence Summaries are contained in F.S. Regs., Part II. and the Staff Manual respectively. Title pages will be prepared in manuscript.

Place	Date	Hour	Summary of Events and Information	Remarks and references to Appendices
	Feb			
SCHERPENBERG	14th	1.0am	Heavy bombardment of sector on right of DURHAM ROAD.	
		1.5pm	S.O.S signal seen by our guns who immediately "stood to" and the following guns opened fire	
			C.T.s on N°1 6 31 D 750 rounds.	
			N°4 on " O 31 A 500 do	
			N°6 on enemy support lines in N 36 B 1000 rounds.	
			N°11 " " " " O 31 C 1500 do	
		1.45am	Teams stood down.	
			It was afterwards reported than an enemy raid had been attempted but which had ended disastrously, the raiding party being either killed, wounded or taken prisoner.	
			All quiet reported until 6pm when bombardment of right sector by enemy artillery commenced lasting for 2 hours. Tost on right of N°6 Position receiving some attention.	
			Fire on enemy communication trenches and roads	O. Whelan IX

Army Form C. 2118.

WAR DIARY
or
INTELLIGENCE SUMMARY.
(Erase heading not required.)

Instructions regarding War Diaries and Intelligence Summaries are contained in F.S. Regs., Part II. and the Staff Manual respectively. Title pages will be prepared in manuscript.

Place	Date	Hour	Summary of Events and Information	Remarks and references to Appendices
SCHERPENBERG	Feb 14th (cont.)		Carried out during the night as usual. Total rounds fired 4,750. Casualties nil.	
	15th		All quiet reported from all gun positions in the line during the day. A German aeroplane reported to have English markings, was hit by anti-aircraft shells and was driven towards enemy lines. Skimming 'No-Man's-Land' it appeared to land just in rear of enemy front line. Our M.G's and artillery immediately fired on it. Have fire carried out at night. Three M.G's being at work on emplacement. Aeroplane position. Section relief carried out. A Sec going in + C Sec to Reser. Casualties Nil.	ChS.
	16th		Quiet throughout morning. In afternoon our artillery bombarded enemy trenches causing some retaliation in the vicinity of S.P.8 Beyond usual indirect fire, nothing to report.	J. Watson Lieut. 47th M.G.C.
			Co. Strength 11 officers 178 O.R.	

Army Form C. 2118.

WAR DIARY
or
INTELLIGENCE SUMMARY.
(Erase heading not required.)

Place	Date 1917	Hour	Summary of Events and Information	Remarks and references to Appendices
SCHERPENBERG	17th Feb		Nothing to Report from line during day. Sustained fire carried out during night on:— Rds + C.T's N30 D88 C.T. 02SD33 N30 B11 C.T. 02Sc 1.4 S.P. N30 D98 Chts. Total rounds fired 6,550.	
	18th		During the day our artillery systematically bombarded enemy wire and trenches. No 1 gun fired on enemy C.T's during night. Spasmodic bombardment by our artillery during night.	
	19th	7.15 PM	A raid in force was attempted by 6th (Connaught) Rangers. Owing to alertness of the enemy it was unsuccessful. M.Gs co-operated by forming barrages on enemy trenches and C.T's as follows:— L'ENFER WOOD 031C47 N30 D63 N30 D98 031A91 HELL FARM (031B) A reserve gun in our front line fired on enemy salient N3bB63	Châteauh? Three

Army Form C. 2118.

WAR DIARY
or
INTELLIGENCE SUMMARY.
(Erase heading not required.)

Instructions regarding War Diaries and Intelligence Summaries are contained in F. S. Regs., Part II. and the Staff Manual respectively. Title pages will be prepared in manuscript.

Place	Date	Hour	Summary of Events and Information	Remarks and references to Appendices
		7.30 AM	to keep down hostile rifle fire. Enemy retaliated & no great strength on KINGSWAY and front line trenches.	
		8.45 AM	line normal. Total rounds fired by 8 guns 25,000. There was a little artillery activity by both sides during afternoon.	
		1 pm.	A small explosion was felt in the line. It appears that the enemy is firing small mine-craters in front of to his strong points for them forming of obstacles in case of an advance by us.	
		5.30 pm to 10.30	No 1 gun fired on N30096 No 5 " " N30B11 } No of rounds 2750.	
			Casualties. 1 OR Killed by rifle fire in front line.	

O/Johnson/Lieut
4/7/7/20

T.134. Wt. W708—776. 500000. 4/15. Sir J. C. & S.

Army Form C. 2118.

WAR DIARY
or
INTELLIGENCE SUMMARY.
(Erase heading not required.)

Instructions regarding War Diaries and Intelligence Summaries are contained in F. S. Regs., Part II. and the Staff Manual respectively. Title pages will be prepared in manuscript.

Place	Date	Hour	Summary of Events and Information	Remarks and references to Appendices.
SCHAEFFENBERG	Feb 20th		Nothing to report during morning. Our artillery heavily bombarded enemy lines during the afternoon. No damage was done by enemy retaliation. S.O.S. was sent up on left sector at 6.15 p.m. Our guns 'stood to' and No. 8 gun fired a few bursts, there being no bombardment & no rifle fire however, the teams stood down at 6.30 p.m. During night No. 7 fired on C.T. 0.25.D or N.30 B.11 " No. 5 " " " " 0.25.c.51 " No. 1 " " " " Total rounds fired H. 250. All quiet reported from line.	4/H/S
	21st		Owing to prevailing wet weather work on trenches, emplacements, dug-out etc has been possible. Indirect fire carried on throughout night as usual. Casualties. Arrivals: Lt Williamson (from leave) Departures 1 O.R. to No. 2 C.C.S. 1 O.R. to No. 15 C.C.S.	4/15

Army Form C. 2118.

WAR DIARY
or
INTELLIGENCE SUMMARY.
(Erase heading not required.)

Instructions regarding War Diaries and Intelligence Summaries are contained in F.S. Regs., Part II. and the Staff Manual respectively. Title pages will be prepared in manuscript.

Place	Date	Hour	Summary of Events and Information	Remarks and references to Appendices
SCHERPENBERG	Feb 22nd		Nothing to report from line. Heavy mist all morning. Indirect fire on L'ENFER WOOD, tracks, roads and communication trenches carried on as usual throughout night.	
	23rd	6.30am	Small trench mortar bombardment during 'stand to' on SP6 and front trenches lasting about 10 minutes.	
		9.15	C Sect started out to relieve. B section returned to huts at 2.30pm.	
		6pm	Shelling of SP6 and SP8 reported. No enemy did any damage to gun positions.	
		9pm	Three green rockets observed, fired from enemy front line. Each rocket split into two. Indirect fire carried on as usual.	
			Casualties 1 O.R. arrived from BASE. Strength 4 Offrs. 11 Offs. 178 O.R.	

Army Form C. 2118.

WAR DIARY
or
INTELLIGENCE SUMMARY.
(Erase heading not required.)

Place	Date	Hour	Summary of Events and Information	Remarks and references to Appendices
	24th		All quiet apart from all active in line except for slight bombardment on extreme left.	
		6pm.	A variety of green rockets were let off from German lines this being our S.O.S signal, teams 'stood to' for a short period but did not open fire. Indirect fire on O25 D, O25 A carried out throughout night. Casualties. Nil.	
	25th		Nothing to report. Indirect fire carried out on following targets. OCEAN TRENCH WENFER WOOD ROADS in O25A Total Rounds fired 3,000. Casualties. 1 OR departure to 15 C.C.S.	

Army Form C. 2118.

WAR DIARY
or
INTELLIGENCE SUMMARY.
(Erase heading not required.)

Ref 28 S.W.2 (edition 4A)

Instructions regarding War Diaries and Intelligence Summaries are contained in F.S. Regs., Part II. and the Staff Manual respectively. Title pages will be prepared in manuscript.

Place	Date	Hour	Summary of Events and Information	Remarks and references to Appendices
SCHERPENBERG	26th		All quiet reported from line. Indirect fire carried out as usual. Work on trenches, anti-aircraft positions, emplacements and dug-outs carried on. Casualties. 1 O.R. arrived from 15 C.C.S	chh.
	27th		Nothing to report. Gun sustained throughout night on OCEAN TRENCH, OCCULT AVE, ROADS etc in O2SA.	chh.
	28th g. Nav.		B Sect relieved D section who returned to rest. Activity in the line much less normal. Indirect fire carried out throughout night on L'ENFER WOOD and OCEAN TRENCH. Hostile rounds fired 2000. Casualties. NIL	chh.

C Nelson Lieut
4th MMG CoY

WAR DIARY
FOR MONTH OF MARCH, 1917.

VOLUME 12

UNIT:- No. 4 / Machine Gun Compy.

Vol XI

Army Form C. 2118.

WAR DIARY
or
INTELLIGENCE SUMMARY.
(Erase heading not required.)

Ref. Map WYTSCHAETE 28 S.W 2 (Edition 4A)

Instructions regarding War Diaries and Intelligence Summaries are contained in F. S. Regs., Part II. and the Staff Manual respectively. Title pages will be prepared in manuscript.

Place	Date 1917	Hour	Summary of Events and Information	Remarks and references to Appendices
SCHERPENBERG	MARCH 1ST.		Nothing to report from guns in line during daylight.	
			At 7pm N°1, 5 & 7 guns co-operated with the artillery in forming a 'box barrage' to support a small raiding party. The guns opened at 7pm on the following targets. L'ENFER WOOD OCCULT AVE. OCCUR TRENCH.	
			At 7.15pm two red rockets were sent up from enemy lines and N° 6, 10 & 11 guns opened fire on these targets.	
			At 7.20pm all guns ceased fire. Total no. of rounds fired 1,650. Throughout night ordinary fire was maintained on roads and tracks in rear of enemy lines.	
			Casualties	ChS
			3 O.R. joined from BASE DEPOT.	
	2nd		All quiet reported from line. Indirect fire on OCCUR TR. (O31A+B) OCEAN LANE (O21B) and L'ENFER WOOD carried out throughout night. Coy. Strength 11 officers 181 O.R.	Ch.Willson ?/?Pickler

Army Form C. 2118.

WAR DIARY
or
INTELLIGENCE SUMMARY.
(Erase heading not required.)

Instructions regarding War Diaries and Intelligence Summaries are contained in F.S. Regs., Part II. and the Staff Manual respectively. Title pages will be prepared in manuscript.

Place	Date 1917	Hour	Summary of Events and Information	Remarks and references to Appendices
SCHERPENBERG	MARCH 3rd		All quiet reported from line. Indirect fire carried out on the following targets during night:- L'ENFER WOOD STRONG POINT (O25A) OCCUR TRENCH (O31A) Work on trench repair & construction, maintenance of emplacement & improvement of dug-outs carried out throughout night	OWS
	4th		There is nothing to report from the line. Activity on part of the enemy has been below normal. Harass indirect fire carried on throughout night. Working parties obtained from the Infantry utilized for constructing trench joining up Nos 6 & 11 positions and deepening trenches at No 1 emplacement. Casualties. 1 O.R. 10 BASE ineffectual.	C/Wilson Lieut M/175 Co

Army Form C. 2118.

WAR DIARY
or
INTELLIGENCE SUMMARY.
(Erase heading not required.)

Instructions regarding War Diaries and Intelligence Summaries are contained in F. S. Regs., Part II. and the Staff Manual respectively. Title pages will be prepared in manuscript.

Place	Date 1917	Hour	Summary of Events and Information	Remarks and references to Appendices
SCHERPENBERG	MARCH 5th		The relief of sections in line carried out during morning	
			D Sect relieving "C"	
			C " " B	
			B " " A	
			A " to rest.	
		1.30 pm.	Reliefs complete 1.30 pm.	
			Guns fired at night as follows.	
			No 1 Gun on L'ENFER WOOD	
			No 5 " " OCCUR TRENCH } Total rounds fired 1500.	
			No 7 " " O25 D68	
			Much work was done during the night on building trenches etc	
			Casualties :- Nil.	

T2134. Wt. W708—776. 500000. 4/15. Sir J.C.&S.

WAR DIARY
or
INTELLIGENCE SUMMARY.
(Erase heading not required.)

Army Form C. 2118.

Place	Date	Hour	Summary of Events and Information	Remarks and references to Appendices
SCHERPENBERG.	March 6th		Nothing to report from line except for some hostile machine gun SPG. At night usual fire arrived out on enemy C.T.s & roads of communication.	
			Work on trenches at KINGSWAY and FLUFFY POST carried on, and dugout at KINGSWAY nearly completed. Casualties 1 O.R. wounded.	O.W.
	7th		All quiet reported from all guns in the line. Usual indirect fire carried out during night, 3500 rounds being fired. Casualties. NIL.	O.W.
	8th		All quiet reported during morning.	
	3.30pm		Enemy heavily bombarded our front line and strong points. Bombardment lasted 3 hours during which time all teams stood 'to'. 4 guns were fired to ensure that they were in working order.	O.W.
	6pm		A large fire was observed to rear of enemy line	

Army Form C. 2118.

WAR DIARY
or
INTELLIGENCE SUMMARY.
(Erase heading not required.)

Instructions regarding War Diaries and Intelligence Summaries are contained in F. S. Regs., Part II. and the Staff Manual respectively. Title pages will be prepared in manuscript.

Place	Date 1917	Hour	Summary of Events and Information	Remarks and references to Appendices
SCHERPENBERG	MARCH 8th		approximately at HELL FARM. Four guns were at once turned on to this. From 7.30pm to midnight 'all quiet' reported. Casualties.	
	9th		1 O.R. wounded.	OMS
		4AM.	At HAM. enemy bombarded front line, strong points and C.T's.	
		4.5PM	S.O.S. signal sent up from our front line. All guns immediately opened fire on enemy front line, support line and C.T's. according to DEFENCE SCHEME.	
		5.15AM	NORMAL resumed and guns ceased fire. It afterwards appeared that four large enemy parties attempted to raid our trenches but were beaten off without entering + forced to retire, chiefly through M.G. fire. Two prisoners were taken and several bodies left	M/S

T.134. Wt. W708—776. 500000. 4/15. Sir J. C. & S.

WAR DIARY
or
INTELLIGENCE SUMMARY.
(Erase heading not required.)

Army Form C. 2118.

Place	Date	Hour	Summary of Events and Information	Remarks and references to Appendices
(Continued)			In NO-MANS-LAND. Total rounds fired 32,000. The enemy bombardment damaged No 2 Emplacement and trench at FLUFFY POST but no great harm was done. Strength Officers 11 O.R. 191 } Total Officers 11 O.R. 178. (attached) 7	ChS
	10th		Section relief carried out 9.15 a.m. A Sect relieving D in position 6,7,10 & 11 D " " C " " 3,4,5 C in positions 5,7,8 & 12 C Sect to Camp B remaining in positions 1,2,8 & 9 Nothing to report by day.	
		5.30pm	Wanted moving of troops behind PETIT BOIS. All teams stood to throughout night but apart from slight shelling by 77mm	6/7/photo

WAR DIARY
or
INTELLIGENCE SUMMARY.
(Erase heading not required.)

Army Form C. 2118.

Place	Date	Hour	Summary of Events and Information	Remarks and references to Appendices
SCHERPENBERG	10th		and some m.g. fire at 3 AM (on 11th) nothing to report. Indirect fire was carried out on L'ENFER WOOD OCCULT AVE Casualties NIL. 1 O.R. to Base Depot — inefficient.	
	11th		Except for some artillery & trench mortar activity nothing to report by day. All quiet reported throughout night. Guns fired on enemy tracks and roads throughout night as usual.	9/4/15
	12th		Nothing to report from line during morning	
		12.30pm	Relief of teams in line by 109th M.G. Coy. 36th Division commenced.	
		2.30pm	Relief reported complete. Teams relieved return to H.Q SCHERPENBERG.	

WAR DIARY
or
INTELLIGENCE SUMMARY.
(Erase heading not required.)

Army Form C. 2118.

Place	Date	Hour	Summary of Events and Information	Remarks and references to Appendices
	1917 March			
	12th (cont'd)	4.30pm	Camps, transport lines etc at SCHERPENBERG handed over to 49th M.G. Coy	
		5.30pm	Company fallen in and started out for PIEBROUCK. Route taken SCHERPENBERG - MONT ROUGE - MONT VIDAIGNE - BERTHEN - PIEBROUCK.	
		8.45pm	Coy arrived PIEBROUCK.	
		9.15pm	Coy completely settled in billets. Casualties. 2.O.R (att. for work) returned to unit.	ok/s
PIEBROUCK	13th		Morning spent cleaning up personnel etc Afternoon parades for cleaning up equipment, gun equipment etc. 1 O.R to No 2. C.C.S.	ok/s
do	14th		Morning spent in cleaning guns, limbers etc.	
		9.30pm	Coy. Armourer inspected all guns, rifles etc. Casualties NIL.	ok/s
do	15th		Parades as follows:- 9.30 - 10.30 A.M. Kit Inspection 10.30 - 11.30 " Mechanism	ok/s

WAR DIARY
or
INTELLIGENCE SUMMARY.
(Erase heading not required.)

Army Form C. 2118.

Place	Date	Hour	Summary of Events and Information	Remarks and references to Appendices
RIEBROUCK	15th	11.30 – 12.30	Shuffling.	
		2 pm – 3 pm.	Lecture on { Combined Rifle & Bracketing Fire { Verticale Searching	CWS.
			Casualty. 1 O.R. from No 2 C.C.C.	
	16.		Parade as follows	
		9.30 – 10.30 A.M.	Immediate Action	
		10.30 – 11.30 A.M.	C.O.'s Inspection of company	
		11.30 A.M – 12.30 PM	Triangle of Error.	
		2 PM – 3 PM	Lecture on Range. Cards for attack + defence.	CWS
			Signaller training separately in Station work.	
			Coy Strength 11 officers 169 O.R.	CJ Walker Scott Lt. H. H. Syle

WAR DIARY
or
INTELLIGENCE SUMMARY.
(Erase heading not required.)

Army Form C. 2118.

Place	Date	Hour	Summary of Events and Information	Remarks and references to Appendices
PIEBROUCK	March 1917 17		St Patricks Day, and holiday for Brigade. Church Parade for R.C.s at BERTHEN at 9.30 A.M. Company Sports held in afternoon.	Ch/15
do	18th		Church Parade as follows:- R.C. Mass at BERTHEN at 11 A.M. C of E. 10.45 A.M. at Coy H.Q. Non Conformists 11.45 A.M. During afternoon mule race and Inter-Section football were run played have been unavoidably held over.	Ch/15
do	19th		Parade as follows:- 9:30 - 10.30 A.M. Gym frise 10.30 - 11.30 A.M. Immediate action 11.30 - 12.30 P.M. Beet Alley by machine 2 - 3 P.M. Lecture on "Indication & recognition of Targets".	[signature]

Army Form C. 2118.

WAR DIARY
or
INTELLIGENCE SUMMARY.
(Erase heading not required.)

Place	Date	Hour	Summary of Events and Information	Remarks and references to Appendices
PIEBROUCK	19		Casualties: Arr. 2 O.R. rejoined from M.G. Course at CAMIERS. Dep. 1 Off - 2 O.R. to M.G. School CAMIERS.	O/h/K
do	20th		Parade during morning as follows:- 9.30 - 10.30 AM Gun drill 10.30 - 11.30 Immediate action 11.30 - 12.30 PM Belt Filling by machine Casualties. 1 O.R. arrived from BASE DEPOT	O/h/K
do	21st		Parade as follows:- 9.30 - 12.30 TB Sect. on range for M.G. & revolver practice. Remainder of Coy. route march. 2.30 - 3.30 PM. Cleaning and oiling guns. Casualties. 1 O.R. evac to No. 2 C.C.S. sick.	absent 4/15 T213

Army Form C. 2118.

WAR DIARY
or
INTELLIGENCE SUMMARY.
(Erase heading not required.)

Instructions regarding War Diaries and Intelligence Summaries are contained in F.S. Regs., Part II. and the Staff Manual respectively. Title pages will be prepared in manuscript.

Place	Date	Hour	Summary of Events and Information	Remarks and references to Appendices
	1919 MARCH			
PIEBROUCK	22nd	Parade. 9.30 - 10AM.	Cleaning and Oiling all guns & Tripods	
		10AM - 11AM	Cleaning of equipment, Service Dress etc.	
		11.15 AM	C.O's Inspection	
		11.30	The Company proceeded to undergoing an inspection by G.O.C. 2nd Army.	ch.h
			Crawls.	
			1 O.R. (previously attacked Bn H.Q.) reported to duty.	
do.	23rd	Parade 9.30 AM to 10.30 AM.	Cleaning and oiling limbers	
		10.30 AM to 12.30 P.M.	C Section on range.	
			Remainder of Coy, mechanism and instruction in Boss & Stroud.	
		2pm to 3pm.	Lecture on "Points to be attended to before, during and after firing."	
		Coy Strength.	11 offs. 141 O.Rs	
		Casualties.	1 O.R evac sick to No 2 C.C.S LT Swatfield to England from Cambers on special 10 days leave.	

T.J.134. Wt. W708—776. 500000. 4/15. Sir J.C. & S.

WAR DIARY
or
INTELLIGENCE SUMMARY.
(Erase heading not required.)

Army Form C. 2118.

Place	Date 1914	Hour	Summary of Events and Information	Remarks and references to Appendices
PIEBROUCK	March 24th		Parades. 9.30 AM to 10.30 AM. Gun drill	
			10.30 PM to 11.30 " Immediate action	
			11.30 " to 12.30 P.M. Belt filling by machine	
			3 P.M. Coy. Parade	C/M
			Summer Time adopted at 11 P.M.	
	25th		Parades. 7 AM to 8 AM. Squad drill and physical drill	
			Church Parades.- R.C. Mass at BERTHEN 10 A.M.	
			C.of E. at Coy H.Q. 11.45 P.M.	
			Nonconformists at 10.30 A.M.	
			Reservations. N°13214 L/Cpl JAMIESON J. deprived of lance-stripe for	
			(i) refusing to obey an order.	
			ii. Being absent from parade at 7 A.M.	
			Promotion. N°15404 Pte WILLIAMS E to be L/Cpl.	C/M O/N/others W/H C/plas

Army Form C. 2118.

WAR DIARY
or
INTELLIGENCE SUMMARY.
(Erase heading not required.)

Instructions regarding War Diaries and Intelligence Summaries are contained in F.S. Regs., Part II. and the Staff Manual respectively. Title pages will be prepared in manuscript.

Place	Date	Hour	Summary of Events and Information	Remarks and references to Appendices
PIERREGOUT	26th	Parade.	7am to 8am Physical Drill & squad drill	
			9.30 – 10.30 Musketry	
			10.30 – 11.30 Immediate Action	
			11.30 – 12.30 Gun drill.	
			b Sect on range from 9.30 am to 12.30 pm	
			2pm to 3pm Lecture on Trench Warfare (defence)	
	27th	Parade.	7am to 8am Physical Drill and squad drill	
			9.30am to 12.30pm C . D Sections on range	
			A . B " { Belt filling, Snipping, Cleaning guns etc "Selection and Occupation"	
			2pm to 3pm Lecture on "Selection and Occupation of gun position."	
			During the day 3 officers reconnoitred sector of trenches to be taken over by Coy.	

WAR DIARY
or
INTELLIGENCE SUMMARY.
(Erase heading not required.)

Army Form C. 2118.

Place	Date	Hour	Summary of Events and Information	Remarks and references to Appendices
PIERROUCK	28th		Parade.	
		7AM – 8AM	Physical Drill & Squad Drill	
		9.30am – 12.30am.	{ A Sect Range work { Remainder of Coy, Gun drill, Triangle of Error and Kit Inspection	
		2 pm – 3 pm	Lecture on "Work & Routine in Trenches".	
			Casualties 3 officers proceeded to reinforce new sector. 1 O.R. rejoined Company from M.G. Course.	O/L/S
do	29th		Parade	
		7AM – 8AM	Physical Drill – Squad Drill.	
		9.30 – 12.30	Attack practice.	
		2pm – 3pm	{ D Section rangework { Remainder cleaning Guns etc.	
		8pm – 11pm	Company Concert.	

Walsh Lieut
Officer Coy

Army Form C. 2118.

WAR DIARY
or
INTELLIGENCE SUMMARY.
(Erase heading not required.)

Instructions regarding War Diaries and Intelligence Summaries are contained in F.S. Regs., Part II. and the Staff Manual respectively. Title pages will be prepared in manuscript.

Place	Date	Hour	Summary of Events and Information	Remarks and references to Appendices
RIEBROUCK	March 30th		Parade. 7am-8am. Physical Drill. 9.30am-12.30pm. Cleaning up of limber harness etc. 2pm-3pm. Coy. Parade in full marching order for inspection by C.O.	C/J.S.
SCHERPENBERG	31st	10.15am.	Company paraded to march to SCHERPENBERG.	
		10.25am.	Company left RIEBROUCK.	
		1.30pm.	Arrived at SCHERPENBERG, and taking over former camp, during afternoon preparations were made for taking over trenches.	C/J.S.

O.H. Bushell Lieut
4th M.G.Co

WAR DIARY FOR MONTH OF APRIL, 1917.

VOLUME:- 13

UNIT:- H.Q. Machine Gun Corp.

Army Form C. 2118.

WAR DIARY
or
INTELLIGENCE SUMMARY.
(Erase heading not required.)

Instructions regarding War Diaries and Intelligence Summaries are contained in F. S. Regs., Part II. and the Staff Manual respectively. Title pages will be prepared in manuscript.

Place	Date	Hour	Summary of Events and Information	Remarks and references to Appendices
	April			
Pioneer Farm	1st		Relief of Hqt M.G. Coy in WYTSCHETE Sector carried out.	
		8:15AM	A,C,D Sections paraded at SCHERPENBERG and marched to KEMMEL via LA CLYTTE.	
		9:30AM	Arrived LA CLYTTE and guide for position in trenches picked up.	
		11:45AM	Relief reported complete.	
			H.Q and B Section at Pioneer Farm.	
			Nothing to report from line during remainder of day.	Ch/ts
do	2nd		Nothing to report from line during day. The following work was got in hand in the line.	
			D Sect. SASKATCHEWAN Right Gun { Repair of timber and trench traverse	
			do LEFT GUN { Completion of dug outs and splinter proofs	
			FORT CALGARY. General cleaning up of emplacements etc.	
			C Sect. BRYKEME Right Gun { Improvement of parapets, upkeep of VIERSTRAAT SWITCH	
			do LEFT do { and emplacements during. Building of new emplacement.	
			FOSSE do Ammunition succern	
			PAPROT do	Ch/tam A/M/tb

WAR DIARY or INTELLIGENCE SUMMARY

Army Form C. 2118.

Place	Date	Hour	Summary of Events and Information	Remarks and references to Appendices
PIONEER FARM	2nd (continued)		A Section VAN KEEP Gun (Building of latrines, drainage of trenches and dug-outs. Repairs to trenches and trench boards	
			Fort HALIFAX Gun { Cleaning up of emplacements.	
			MOUND Gun {	
			DESINET F.M Gun. Repair of emplacement in VIERSTRAAT SWITCH	
			Firing early morning and night 2nd/3rd the following targets were fired on.	
			DESINET F.M Gun fired on O19A 83 and K.F.00 N24D 14	
			MOUND " " " HOSACE { TOTAL No. of ROUNDS 3,150
			FOSSE " " " O19A 5½	
			Parade for B. Sect.	
			9.30am – 12.30pm General cleaning of gun equipment, drills etc	Obs.
			2.00pm – 3.00pm Mechanism	
	3rd		Guns in line numbered as follows	
			1 PARROT TRENCH Gun, 4 FOSSE Gun 7 VAN KEEP 10 FORT SASKATCHEWAN (L)
			2 BATTERIE LEFT do. 5 DESINET do. 8 THE MOUND 11 " (R)
			3 " RIGHT do. 6 FORT HALIFAX do. 9 FORT CALGARY.	

Army Form C. 2118.

WAR DIARY
or
INTELLIGENCE SUMMARY.
(Erase heading not required.)

Instructions regarding War Diaries and Intelligence Summaries are contained in F.S. Regs., Part II. and the Staff Manual respectively. Title pages will be prepared in manuscript.

Place	Date	Hour	Summary of Events and Information	Remarks and references to Appendices
PIONEER FARM	30 June		Work was carried out in the lines as usual and the following fire carried out.	
			Gun no 5. TARGET BLACK COT & HOSPICE N° of Rds 150.	
			N° 1 O13C3 8½ 2000	
		5.30pm	A bombardment by our artillery of enemy trenches, support trenches and communication trenches started and lasted until	
		6.40pm		
			Enemy retaliated strongly on YAN KEEP obtaining a direct hit on both M.G. dug-out and emplacement.	
			Parade for B Section.	
		9.30 AM - 12.30 PM	Parade in fighting order to proceed to Transport lines to clean limbers and contents.	
		2.00 pm - 3.00 pm	Revl wire parade.	
		4.30 pm onwards	Working parties	
				OW.

O Wilson Lieut
4th M.G. Co.

Army Form C. 2118.

WAR DIARY
or
INTELLIGENCE SUMMARY.
(Erase heading not required.)

Place	Date	Hour	Summary of Events and Information	Remarks and references to Appendices
PIONEER FARM	4th		There was retaliation in morning to our bombardment of last night. Much work was done during day and night. A little indirect fire was carried out from 9pm to 1am on usual targets.	
		5.3	Another bombardment was carried out by our artillery drawing	
		-but strong retaliation.		
			Casualties 1 O.R. to No 1 C.C.S.	
			1 O.R. to 7th LEINSTERS (inefficient)	
	5th		Nothing to report by day.	
		5.30-	Bombardment carried out as last night.	
		6.45pm		
		8.45pm	Zero hour for raid & carried out by 6th Conne Iush Regt. ZERO plus 1 hour. M.G.s co-operated with artillery in forming box barrage, as follows.	
			No 1 + 3 PETIT BOIS - HOSPICE.	

WAR DIARY
or
INTELLIGENCE SUMMARY.

(Erase heading not required.)

Army Form C. 2118.

Instructions regarding War Diaries and Intelligence Summaries are contained in F.S. Regs., Part II. and the Staff Manual respectively. Title pages will be prepared in manuscript.

Place	Date	Hour	Summary of Events and Information	Remarks and references to Appendices
PIONEER FARM.	5th Combust.		2 + 4 guns F UNNAMED WOOD + HOSPICE to S.E.	
			5.8 " C.T.s in and around HOSPICE + BRICKSTACK	
			9 " PIMPLE	
			10 " NAME TRENCH.	
			Total rounds fired during the hour and a half the enemy trench 30,000.	
			Ruding party remained the enemy trench line slacked down when "all-in" signal was observed at 10·15 P.M.	
			+ ceased at 10:30.	
			Raid reported successful, 21 prisoners being captured.	
			Enemy retaliated on FORT SASKATCHEWAN, VAN KEEP and FOSSE. No material damage done to any position.	
			Casualties. 8 O.R. from BASE DEPOT	
			Strength on APR 213. Officers 11 O.R. 1/4 attached 1 off.	
			[signature] Lieut H/Kt M.G. Co	

Army Form C. 2118.

WAR DIARY
or
INTELLIGENCE SUMMARY.
(Erase heading not required.)

Instructions regarding War Diaries and Intelligence Summaries are contained in F.S. Regs., Part II. and the Staff Manual respectively. Title pages will be prepared in manuscript.

Place	Date	Hour	Summary of Events and Information	Remarks and references to Appendices
PIONEER PARK.	6th		Nothing to report by day. Indirect fire carried out at night on N.24.B. 50.60. N.13.C.60. Ydles Round 1500.	
			Took as usual carried out at night aided by T.E. and working parties from B.9.e.5.	
			Parade for B. Section. Working Parties. Remainder. Kit Inspection + cleaning S.A.A. etc.	O.K.
do.	7th		Nothing to report from 1am until 1.30pm. when a heavy enemy bombardment with gas + tear shells took place. Expecting a counter-raid all teams '1000-1-15' went gun laid on battle line. No 9 gun opened fire sweeping PETIT BOIS and UNNAMED WOOD. The bombardment ceased at 10.30pm no infantry action following. Work + indirect fire carried out as usual.	Abraham Kent

Army Form C. 2118.

WAR DIARY
or
INTELLIGENCE SUMMARY.
(Erase heading not required.)

Instructions regarding War Diaries and Intelligence Summaries are contained in F.S. Regs., Part II. and the Staff Manual respectively. Title pages will be prepared in manuscript.

Place	Date	Hour	Summary of Events and Information	Remarks and references to Appendices
Pioneer Farm.	April 8th	1-9pm	No activity to report during daylight. A very heavy bombardment took place on 21st Divisional front on left during and throughout night. Cars roads at OIG B 05 60 OI3 C/12, were kept under fire of no 1 & 8 guns. Much work was carried on. Section in reserve were retained during night for working parties. Casualties. Nil.	Chs.
do.	9th		Working to report by day. Indirect fire and work carried on as usual. Reserve Section: Parade. 9.30 - 10.30 Immediate action. 10.30 - 11.30 Belt Filling by Hand. 11.30 - 12.30 Stoppages. Casualties. Nil.	

O.L. Wilson Lieut
4 M.M.G.Co

WAR DIARY
or
INTELLIGENCE SUMMARY.
(Erase heading not required.)

Army Form C. 2118.

Place	Date	Hour	Summary of Events and Information	Remarks and references to Appendices
PIONEER F^M	10th		Nothing to report from line. Guns fired as usual during night on enemy ration parties, communication trenches, roads & transport. There were some enemy M.G. retaliation on the Bayneres Guns. Casualties. 2 OR to No 2. C.C.S (NEURASTHENIA)	O.W.R
do	11th	9AM	4 guns of "B" Sect. relieved 4 guns of the 19 M.M.G. Battery in the KEMMEL HILL DEFENCES. Relief was complete at 10.45AM when this action came under the orders of G.O.C. 36th Division. Nothing to report from line. Normal work carried on night & day. Fire carried out as follow throughout night. Cross F^h O13c 6.9h O19 a 5.9h C T's Trenches between BRICKSTACK & HOSPICE. KAME TRENCH. Casualties. NIL	O. Watson Lieut Lt. 4th MMG

WAR DIARY
or
INTELLIGENCE SUMMARY.
(Erase heading not required.)

Army Form C. 2118.

Place	Date	Hour	Summary of Events and Information	Remarks and references to Appendices
PIONEER FM	Aug 11th		Nothing to report other than some activity on part of our heavy artillery + hostile shelling of M.G. position. Gun fire as usual throughout night on customary targets. Harassing parties as usual. Casualties Nil.	Chr
	12		Nothing to report from line.	
	13	3-4pm	Enemy's battery just behind PIONEER FARM sent 5.9 H.E. No damage was done to H.Q although billets had to be evacuated and all men sent to reserve line of trench.	
		6.30	Billets again had to be evacuated on account of hostile fire. Indirect fire + wants as usual. Casualties Nil.	
			Coy Strength 11 officers. 172 O.R + 1 O.R. attached.	

[signature]
Lt Col
4th MGC [?]

Army Form C. 2118.

WAR DIARY
or
INTELLIGENCE SUMMARY.
(Erase heading not required.)

Place	Date	Hour	Summary of Events and Information	Remarks and references to Appendices
PIONEER FM	14th		Nothing to report from line. Enemy's fire and ours worn on throughout night. Parades for men out of trenches + working parties. Casualties NIL.	9/15
	15th		Nothing to report from line.	
		2.30pm	H.Q. trenches were shelled with H.E. + Tear shell. bombardment lasted 15 minutes. No damage done. Throughout night guns as follows fired.— No 1. on OIGA 5a2/b No 5. on UNNAMED ROAD to HOOGE No 10. on NAME TRENCH. Total rounds fired 5000. Work as usual carried on day + night. Casualties NIL.	

Christison Lieut
a/Adjt 9. E.

WAR DIARY or INTELLIGENCE SUMMARY

Army Form C. 2118

Ref Sheet 28 SW Edition 7A

Place	Date	Hour	Summary of Events and Information	Remarks and references to Appendices
PIONEER F[?].	17th		Activity normal in line. Indirect fire carried out at night on communication trenches and some retaliation by hostile M.G. was noticed but no damage was done. The hostile gun appeared to have three snipers which covered our whole front. It fired from 11.15 pm to about 12 m. nght. Strength 3 O.R. from BASE DEPOT.	chh.
do.	18th		Nothing to report from the beyond repeated attempts fire from what affected our front line was maintained on the HOSPICE (O19A), BRICKSTACKS (O19A), NAME TRENCH (N18D) and also on various communication trenches. The enemy were unusually quiet throughout night. Strength Dinane.	
			Losses 1 O.R. to BASE DEPOT (unlikely ever to become an efficient machine gunner) 1 O.R. to No. 2 C.C.S. invalid sick. 1 O.R. granted 10 days special leave to U.K.	

[signature] Lieut
[signature] Cov.

Army Form C. 2118

WAR DIARY or INTELLIGENCE SUMMARY

(Erase heading not required.)

Ref. Sheet 28 SW Edition 11.A

Place	Date	Hour	Summary of Events and Information	Remarks and references to Appendices
PIONEER FARM.	19th	9.30AM	The Coy was relieved by the 48th MG Coy. Guides from each gun position in the line met at KEMMEL CHATEAU and conveyed relieving teams to the gun positions.	
		11.45AM	Relief reported complete to Brigade H.Q. On relief, the company marched to KLONDYKE FARM. N19C.05 where Coy. H.Q. were established at Kemmel. A, C, & D Sections billeted in barns etc. B Section being still in position in KEMMEL HILL DEFENCES.	O/S.
		2-5pm	Cleaning up of guns & material	
KLONDYKE FM.	20th		Day spent in bathing, cleaning up limbers, guns, spare parts, and service stores. Casualties NIL. Coy strength shown of AFB 213. Officers 11 O.R. 171 attached 1 Sick (included in above Total) 5	CNelson Lieut 4th MG Coy

1875 Wt. W5913/826 1,000,000 4/15 J.B.C. & A. A.D.S.S./Forms/C. 2118.

Army Form C. 2118

WAR DIARY
or
INTELLIGENCE SUMMARY
(Erase heading not required.)

Instructions regarding War Diaries and Intelligence Summaries are contained in F.S. Regs., Part II. and the Staff Manual respectively. Title Pages will be prepared in manuscript.

Ref. Map 28 SW & A. H.A.

Place	Date	Hour	Summary of Events and Information	Remarks and references to Appendices
MORBECQUE	FM 25th to 28th		Whilst in Support area the Company trained daily in the following subjects: Physical drill, Squad drill with Smoke helmets, Squad drill, Gun drill and named gun subjects (mechanism etc.) Stoppages. Musketry was practiced every day. Towards the end of the period, men fired on m.q. range and Smoketers carrying loads to accustom them to revolver range; Route-marched across country carrying guns etc. Routes in route advance were examined. Model of the enemy position in whole company examined. Fitting pack-saddlery. Squares 07. 13. 19. 25. 31. 14. 20. 26. 32. M. 16. 24. 30. 36. U. 1. 2. 3. 8. 9. A series of lectures were given on the 26th 27th + 28th inst. on "Heavy Artillery," "Co-operation between Infantry and Flying Corps" and "Light Artillery." All officers and N.C.Os off duty attended. In order to ensure co-operation between M.G. Sections and Battalions the Company was distributed amongst battalions as follows:- A Sect Enid 1st R MUNSTER FUS. B " " 5th CONNAUGHT RANGERS C " " 6th R. IRISH REGt D " " 7th LEINSTER R.C. Regt. Who were done so	O'Nolan Lieut

Army Form C. 2118

WAR DIARY
or
INTELLIGENCE SUMMARY
(Erase heading not required.)

Instructions regarding War Diaries and Intelligence Summaries are contained in F.S. Regs., Part II. and the Staff Manual respectively. Title Pages will be prepared in manuscript.

Place	Date	Hour	Summary of Events and Information	Remarks and references to Appendices
Kemmel Fr.	25th to 29th		All M.G. officers would learn & get acquainted with officers of the battalion they would work with in any forthcoming operations. The following are casualties during the period (21st to 29th inclusive) affecting normal role of Company. Arrivals 25th .... 1 O.R. from 2 C.C.S. 28th .... 1 O.R. " 15 C.C.S. (formerly evacuated) Departures 26th .... 1 O.R. to 53 C.C.S. 27th .... 1 O.R. to 53 C.C.S. Strength shown on AB 213 21.4.17. 11 officers 112 O.R. In addition to above casualties affecting effective strength 25th .... 1 O.R. (attached to Coy) gone to 53 C.C.S. 26th .... 1 O.R. to Div. Signallers course. 9 O.R. in hospital (not evacuated), of which suffering from trench fever.	Officers leave ?? on ??

1875 Wt. W593/826 1,000,000 4/15 J.B.C. & A. A.D.S.S./Forms/C. 2118.

Army Form C. 2118

WAR DIARY
or
INTELLIGENCE SUMMARY
(Erase heading not required.)

Instructions regarding War Diaries and Intelligence Summaries are contained in F.S. Regs., Part II. and Staff Manual respectively. Title Pages will be prepared in manuscript.

Place	Date	Hour	Summary of Events and Information	Remarks and references to Appendices
Monchiette Fm.	3ck		Coy paraded for training as follows:-	
		7-8 AM	Short Route March and Physical Drill.	
		9.30-10.30	Gun drill during this hour N.C.Os were trained in instructing	
		10.30-11.30	Belt filling by machine.	
		11.30-12.30	A.C. & D Section fireward co-operation in attack. Covering fire etc.	
		2-3pm	Signalling.	
			B Section were relieved at 12pm by 108th M.G. Coy. Relief reported complete at 3.15pm. Casualties NIL.	obs

O. Hudson Lieut
A/A M.G.O.O.

WAR DIARY:
---------oOo---------

VOLUME:- 14

FOR MONTH OF MAY, 1917.

UNIT:- 47th Machine Gun Company

Vol 13

WAR DIARY
or
INTELLIGENCE SUMMARY
(Erase heading not required.)

Army Form C. 2118

Place	Date	Hour	Summary of Events and Information	Remarks and references to Appendices
KEMMEL FARM	May 1st		Training as usual throughout day in Physical exer., Squad drill, stripping, map reading, making of range-finders and signalling. Inspection. 1 O.R. to No 2 C.C.S.	OLD
	2nd		Training in route marketing, physical brill, squad drill, gun drill, and attack practice, in range-finder, and signalling. The stampfut were congratulated by the C.O. on the smartness of their turnout. Arrivals 6 O.R. from 108 M.G. Coy (inter Coy transfer) 1 O.R. " 104th Stationary H.	OLD
	3rd		Parades as follows:- 7.00 - 8.00 A.M. Short route march. Physical drill, + squad drill. 9.30 - 10.30 A.M. Kit inspection. 10.30 - 11.30 A.M. Limbers, Ammunition + belts cleaned. 11.30 - 12.30 Preparation for trenches 2.00 - 3.0 P.M. Semaphore. Departure 1 O.R. to 53rd C.C.S.	OLD

Army Form C. 2118

WAR DIARY
or
INTELLIGENCE SUMMARY

(Erase heading not required.)

Rtn Shaw 28 S.H.

Place	Date	Hour	Summary of Events and Information	Remarks and references to Appendices
KLONDYKE Fm.	4th		Further preparation for trenches, all material being thoroughly cleaned etc. Guns fitted and prepared.	
			Casualties. 1 O.R. to No 2 C.C.S. 2 O.R. to batt. Cert Stretcher course.	
			Strength shown on APP. 243 Officers 11 O.R. 198 (including 11 sick not evacuated.)	O.h.W.
PIONEER FM.	5th		The Company relieved the 48th M.G. Coy in same sector (N18) Coy. H.Q at PIONEER FARM. Relief orders shewing distribution of Sections in the line attached. Relief reported completed to Bn H.Q. at 12.45 P.M. Nothing to report during afternoon.	Ref APPEN. A
		6.50 p.m.	Enemy commenced shelling back area with H.E. and shrapnel. Many 5.9 and 4.2 shells fell around PIONEER and R.E. FARMS.	
		8.30 p.m.	An H.E. shell set fire to R.E. FARM causing large conflagration	
		9 p.m.	Shelling ceased except for occasional shrapnel over R.E. FARM.	
		1.30- 2.15 AM	Enemy repeated his bombardment of our billets , surrounding area.	O.W.Shaw Lieut
		3.30-4 AM.	Bombardment repeated.	

Army Form C. 2118

WAR DIARY
or
INTELLIGENCE SUMMARY
(Erase heading not required.)

Instructions regarding War Diaries and Intelligence Summaries are contained in F.S. Regs., Part II. and the Staff Manual respectively. Title Pages will be prepared in manuscript.

Place	Date	Hour	Summary of Events and Information	Remarks and references to Appendices
PIONEER FARM	5 May continued		During the night a recont. of the movement carried by the enemy this wire laid in trouble transport according to guns in Company "Barrage Scheme" in event of attack. No 10 gun fired 500 rounds on 2nd Army Rest Camp NAME TRENCH (N18) from 9PM to midnight 9hrs. Casualties. Gun went out at 10PM. Relief of teams at VAN KEEP and similar acting to last night All quiet during took place. Fire as follows was carried out from dust onwards. No 10 gun fired 560 Rounds at junction of NAP DRIVE, NAP RESERVE, OCCASION ALLEY (O19c 25 90) there was some enemy M.G. retaliation on the gun. No 9 gun fired 1250 rds at HOSPICE. No retaliation. No 8 " 1500 " X Trench O19A 43	
	6th		During the morning an enemy aeroplane flying low over YORK ROAD was engaged by the MAUSER gun. Casualties 1 OFR. to 3rd Army School of Cookery. Lecturer 1 Officer special leave to U.K.	

J. Wilson Lieut

Army Form C. 2118.

WAR DIARY
or
INTELLIGENCE SUMMARY

(Erase heading not required.)

Instructions regarding War Diaries and Intelligence Summaries are contained in F. S. Regs, Part II. and the Staff Manual respectively. Title pages will be prepared in manuscript.

Hour, Date, Place	Summary of Events and Information	Remarks and references to Appendices
PIONEER FM May 7th 1917	Nothing important by day. Harrat mortar fire carried out as usual. Nos 9, 10 & 11 guns being silenced in retaliation.	ditto.
8th	All quiet by day. Harassed activity by enemy artillery during night.	
11.10 pm	S.O.S. signal fired on right front – guns opened to keep down defence.	
12.30 am	Guns ceased fire.	
9th	Slight activity by enemy artillery during day, increasing in violence during evening. It seems intense at 8.45 pm on left sector.	ditto.
9.10 pm 9.12 pm	S.O.S. signal observed from a company firing line system. Guns opened fire on enemy front line system. A raid attempted by the enemy was repulsed.	
10.15 pm	"Normal" resumed all teams shot down. Only three minutes slight guns firing the enemy fire died off. 32 Hrs rounds	
11.50 pm	Nos 1, 4, 5, 10 & 11 guns co-operated with 6th Bde Royal Irish Ref	

A. Whitelaw Kent

WAR DIARY
or
INTELLIGENCE SUMMARY

(Erase heading not required.)

Army Form C. 2118.

Hour, Date, Place	Summary of Events and Information	Remarks and references to Appendices
PIONEER FRONT 9th (continued)	In order each to worry the enemy the following targets were engaged by the guns:—	
	No. 1 NAME SUPPORT TRENCH } Total Rounds fired	
	NAME DRIVE } 2500	
	NANCY DRIVE	
	No. 4 Trench NANCY SUPPORT — 3000	
	No. 5 X Trenches O.19.c.35.76 — 1000	
	No. 10 NANCY AVENUE H.24.B. — 1000	
	No. 11 FRONT LINE N.24.c + D — 1000	
	Same as above. Hostile fire reported at	
	12.25 midnight. This once attention was called	
	to the fact that immediately following the Red	
	out no doubt an attempted enemy	
	had success.	
	During the attempted enemy raid at 9 pm	Appendix B.
	was heavily shelled. A report by the officer in	
	command 2nd R.J. PHILLIPS. attached (Appendix B.) — own	C.W.

Army Form C. 2118.

WAR DIARY
or
INTELLIGENCE SUMMARY
(Erase heading not required.)

Instructions regarding War Diaries and Intelligence Summaries are contained in F.S. Regs., Part II. and the Staff Manual respectively. Title pages will be prepared in manuscript.

Place	Hour, Date	Summary of Events and Information	Remarks and references to Appendices
FLORETTE FARM	May 10th	Fine day. Am by H.Q & H.Q. Co'y. Section in the afternoon. Wdy complete at 4.20 p.m. HQ marched to SCHERPENBERG and Company settled in billets at 6.10 p.m.	C/b
QUATRE CROIX.	May 11th	Morning spent cleaning up and preparing for further move.	
	2 p.m.	Company left SCHERPENBERG for new rest. Route taken LOCRE – BAILLEUL– METEREN– QUATRE CROIX	
	5.10 p.m.	Co'y arrived QUATRE CROIX	
	5.25 p.m.	Co'y settled in billets and H.Q established. Co'y strength shewn on A.F.B. 213 = 11 off. 193 O.R.	C/W
do. May 12th	9.00 a.m.	Foot Inspection	
	9.30 – 12.30	Cleaning up of harness equipment, guns etc.	C/b
	2 p.m. – 3 p.m.	Semaphore Signalling	
do. May 13th	9.30 a.m.	Parade for Baths.	
	10 a.m.	Foot Inspection	C/b
	11.30 a.m.	C.O.'s inspection	
	2 – 3 p.m.	Signalling lecture to N.C.O's	

WAR DIARY
or
INTELLIGENCE SUMMARY

(Erase heading not required.)

Army Form C. 2118.

Hour, Date, Place	Summary of Events and Information	Remarks and references to Appendices
QUARTE CROIX May 14th	7 - 8 A.M. Physical Exercise etc.	
	9.30 - 10.30 Gun Drill.	
	10.30 - 11.30 Practice in making range-cards	
	11.30 - 12.30 pm Short route march	
	2 - 3 pm Signalling + lecture to N.C.O.s. O/h/o.	
	Arrival 1 O.R. from 53 C.C.S.	
do May 15th	Cleaning of limbers etc.	
7 - 8 A.M.	Foot Inspection	
10 A.M.	General cleaning up and preparation for a	
	route march. 1 O.R. transferred from 1st R. Munster Fusiliers. O/h/o	
WALLON CAPPEL May 16th 1.15 pm	Company paraded at QUARTE CROIX and started for WALLON - CAPPEL. Route - QUARTE CROIX - STRAZEELE - BORRÉ - HAZEBROUCK - LE CINQ - RUES - WALLON CAPPEL.	
4.20 pm	Coy arrived + billets established in MAIRIE	
	2nd Lieut. B. J. Phillips awarded Divisional Parchment for gallant conduct during operations on O.H. Wilson May. 15th Q.k. inst.	

WAR DIARY or INTELLIGENCE SUMMARY

Army Form C. 2118.

Instructions regarding War Diaries and Intelligence Summaries are contained in F.S. Regs., Part II. and the Staff Manual respectively. Title pages will be prepared in manuscript.

(Erase heading not required.)

Hour, Date, Place	Summary of Events and Information	Remarks and references to Appendices
WALLON CAPPEL. May 14.	Morning spent cleaning up and preparing for further trek.	
12.15 pm	Company paraded and moved off. Route taken :- WALLON CAPPEL – EBBLINGHEM – ARQUES – ST OMER – ST MARTIN – AU – LAERT.	
4.40 pm	Time of arrival at ST MATIN-au-LAERT where Company was billeted in Rue de Boulogne. H.Q.	O/h
ST MARTIN-AU-LAERT. May 18th 12.15 pm	Company moved off for training area. Route:- MARTIN-AU-LAERT – TATINGHEM – SETQUES – LUMBRES – BAYENGHEM-LES-SENINGHEM – AFFRINGUES – WATTERDAL.	
3.40 pm	Arrival at WATTERDAL. Coy Strength 11 Off. 194 O.R.	O/h/S
WATTERDAL. May 19th to May 28th	On arrival at Brigade Training Area, training for the offensive was carried out. The first few days were confined to training Section separately in attack, then the Company in attack, the section working separately and also in general with Battalion, and also on general machine gun training.	O/Walton Kent

WAR DIARY
or
INTELLIGENCE SUMMARY

Army Form C. 2118.

Hour, Date, Place	Summary of Events and Information	Remarks and references to Appendices
WATERDAL May 19th To May 28th	The last ten days were Brigade Rest days, in which the whole Company worked with the Brigade. The training found shows laid out to represent WYTSCHAETE sector of enemy trenches and reactions worked south here. Inspector in battalions on the same lines that moved hither of the Brigade were ordered to attack. Let order. Casualties. Strength 22nd 1 OTT to № 2 C.C.S. On Strength 28th 11 O/R. 19+ O/R.	Ch. Wilson / Major

1247 W 3299 200,000 (E) 8/14 J.B.C. & A. Forms/C. 2118/11.

Army Form C. 2118.

WAR DIARY
or
INTELLIGENCE SUMMARY

(Erase heading not required.)

Instructions regarding War Diaries and Intelligence Summaries are contained in F.S. Regs., Part II. and the Staff Manual respectively. Title pages will be prepared in manuscript.

Hour, Date, Place	Summary of Events and Information	Remarks and references to Appendices
WATTERDAL. May 18th to May 28th	The following departures and arrivals took place not affecting nominal returns etc. 20th — 1 off and 3 o.r. to M.G. School 20th — 1 off and 2 o.r. from M.G. School 21st — 3 o.r. from 2nd Army Rest Camp. 22nd — 2 o.r. " " (tatic duty) 23rd — 1 o.r. from course in Cookery. " — 1 o.r. " " of Cookery. " — 1 o.r. leave to U.K. " — 1 o.r. to U.K. (10 days leave)	Ch. Jordan Lieut. 4/Hghrs. O.C.

1247 W 3299 200,000 (E) 8/14 J.B.C.&A. Forms/C. 2118/11.

Army Form C. 2118.

WAR DIARY
or
INTELLIGENCE SUMMARY.
(Erase heading not required.)

Place	Date	Hour	Summary of Events and Information	Remarks and references to Appendices
LONGUENESSE	May 29th	9AM to 8AM	Parade for cleaning harness and limbers.	
		9AM	Coy Parade in fighting order	
		9.15	March to LONGUENESSE commenced. Route taken WATTERDAL – BAYENGHEM – LUMBRES – SETQUES – WISQUES – LONGUENESSE.	
		1.15pm	Time of arrival. Remainder of day spent in cleaning up etc.	Ch/5
WALLON-CAPPEL	May 30th	7-9AM	Cleaning of harness & limbers.	
		9AM	Coy Parade in fitting order.	
		9.15AM	Coy moved off on march to WALLON CAPPEL. Route taken LONGUENESSE – ST OMER – ARQUES – FORT ROUGE – RENESCURE – WALLON CAPPEL.	
		2pm	Coy H.Q established at the MAIRIE WALLON CAPPEL. Remainder of day spent in cleaning kit etc.	
			Casualties — 1 OR from APM (on completion of sentence) & FPN°1 1 OR to No 20 Hospital CAMIERS	

Army Form C. 2118.

WAR DIARY
or
INTELLIGENCE SUMMARY.
(Erase heading not required.)

Rof Hazebrouck HQr 2nd.on SA

Place	Date	Hour	Summary of Events and Information	Remarks and references to Appendices
CLARE CAMP (or BAILLEUL - LOCRE ROAD)	May 31st	1-8AM	Cleaning of billets etc.	
		9:30AM	Coy left WALLON CAPPEL to march to CLARE CAMP. Route taken:	
			WALLON CAPPEL - LA HTE LOGE - BORRÉ - STRAZEELE - BAILLEUL -	
			CLARE CAMP (800x E. of X Rds at CROIX de POPERINGHE.)	
		4.30pm	Time of arrival	
			In spite of trying weather, dusty roads and little heat	
			none fell out during any of these marches.	
			Casualties (not affecting strength)	
			1 OR on leave to UK. (31st May to 9th June — 10 days)	
			Major Casualties during month of May.	
			Arrivals 26 OR	
			Departures 4 OR	
			31st May.	
			Company Strength 9 officers 194 OR	

W Julian Lieut
4th MGC O

Appendix "A"

COMPANY ORDERS
— by —
CAPT. J.W. CLAPHAM
Commanding No. 47. M.G. Coy.

1. DUTIES.—
7-5-1917

ORDERLY OFFICER.   Lieut. C.D. Blackwell
Next for Duty.   Lieut. A.B. Williamson.
ORDERLY SERGEANT.   Sjt. C. Cooper.
Next for Duty.   Cpl. P. Simmons.

2. RELIEF.

No. 47. M.G. Coy. will relieve No. 48. M.G. Coy. in the Line to-morrow. Guides from 48. M.G. Coy. will be at KEMMEL CHATEAU at 10. A.M. All Belt Boxes will be taken over in the Line — consequently only Guns, Tripods and Spare Parts will be taken in. These will be taken in Sections. S.A.A. limbers will go as far as KEMMEL CHATE. Limbers will then return to KEMMELVIEW FARM and assist in transporting Stores etc. to PIONEER FARM.

All Maps, Range Cards, Ammunition and other Trench Stores will be taken over and receipts given for same.

No emplacement will be taken over without a Range Card.

Cpl. H. Smith will detail one Signaller to take over the telephone at the Mound and another to take over that at the FOSSE.

All Teams and Limbers with fall in at 9 A.M. ready to march off when Section Officers think fit.

Section Officers will get details from Section Officers of No. 48. M.G. Coy. as to work being carried on at Emplacements, Reserve Emplacements, Dugouts, etc.

Relief to be completed by 4.00. P.M. and reported in code to H.Q. PIONEER FARM.

After Relief, sections will be disposed as follows:—
"A" Section at No. 9, 10 and 11 Positions, under Lieut. Phillips. H.Q. at THE MOUND.
"B" Section at Nos. 1, 2, 3 and 4 Positions, under Lieut. Dixon. H.Q. at THE FOSSE.
"C" Section in reserve at PIONEER FARM. Indirect Gun Team for VAN KEEP (No. 7) Lieut. Whitehead will take charge of VAN KEEP with his H.Q. at the Fosse. O.C. "C" Section will make his own arrangements as to relieving the team at VAN KEEP Gun.
"D" Section in Centre Sector Nos. 5, 6 and 8 positions, under Lieut. Sheffield. H.Q. at THE MOUND.

Tracing Maps (with Barrage Scheme) will be sent round to Section Officers this evening.

Transport Officer will make his own arrangements as regards taking over of Transport Lines from No. 48. M.G. Coy. as well as M.G. Stores.

Transport Officer will arrange for one Spare Limber and one available S.A.A. Limber and the Officers Mess Cart to be at Company H.Q. at 9:30. A.M. to take Cooks Stores, Officers Mess Stores, Orderly Room Stores, Signalling Stores and Baggage belonging to C.O. and Second-in-command, to PIONEER FARM. They will repeat the journey until all is cleared away. Lieut. BLACKWELL will take over all Billets at PIONEER FARM and all Maps etc. at 9 A.M.

Company S.M. Cpl. Smith, one N.C.O. and five men, will proceed to PIONEER FARM with one first Limber and will unload all Limbers as they arrive from KLONDYKE FARM.

Lieut. Entwistle will superintend the packing of all Stores etc. at KLONDYKE FARM and will be in charge of the remainder of "C" Section under Senior N.C.O.

All Billets will be left clean and tidy by 9 A.M. ready for inspection by orderly officer at that hour.

Transport Officer will arrange for "C" Sections Fighting Limbers to be kept at PIONEER FARM (together with Mules for same) Lieut Entwistle 2nd in command's horse will also be kept at H.Q.

Issues and receipts will be forwarded to H.Q. as soon as possible.

C. Hudson Lieut for Captain.
Commanding
No. 47. M.G. Coy.

APPENDIX "B".

To O.C.
  4/7th M.G. Coy.

Sir,
　With regard to the hostile attack of bombardment at 9.10 pm (9-5-17) I desire specially to call attention to the admirable conduct of No 9 Gun Team [Corporal Anderson, Privates Nicholls, Bringeman, Mooney, Davey & Brock] under most trying conditions; the position being heavily shelled with H.E. for fully 40 minutes. After firing 2000 rounds, the gun casing was pierced in two places by a portion of H.E. Shrapnel. The gun was immediately dismounted & repaired with plasticine, after which it was again mounted & fired a further 500 rounds. For their conduct in the firing & repair of the gun Corporal Anderson and Private Nicholls [No 1] deserve special recognition.

　(Private Bringeman, who at the beginning of the bombardment was at Adv. H.Q. on Ration Duty, worked his way thro' a heavy barrage in order to do duty with his gun team)

N.B: With regard to No 9 position the heavy & concentrated nature of the shelling strongly suggests that the position is one specially registered by the enemy.

B.J. Phillips 2/Lt
　　　　　　　　　For O/C "A" Section
10-5-17.

WAR   DIARY.

FOR   MONTH   OF   JUNE,   1917.

VOLUME:- 15

UNIT:- 14th Machine Gun Company

WAR DIARY
or
INTELLIGENCE SUMMARY.
(Erase heading not required.)

Army Form C. 2118.

Place	Date	Hour	Summary of Events and Information	Remarks and references to Appendices
CLARE CAMP	June 2nd		Day spent in resting and cleaning up generally. The troops were allowed to sleep in late of the camp being moved into fields several hundred of yards away on account of regular hostile shelling	
"	3rd		Day spent in cleaning up all guns etc in preparation for trenches	CHW
		9.30 pm	"B" Section under Lt Dixon and 2 guns of "A" Section under 2nd Lt MERRY left CLARE CAMP to relieve 6 guns of the 48th M.G. Coy in the WYTSCHAETE SECTOR	
		10 pm	Remainder of company left CLARE CAMP for KLONDYKE FARM	
KLONDYKE FARM	3rd	4.15 am	Relief about complete. Positions taken over :- B Sect - FORT CALGARY, FORT HALIFAX, DESIRET, THE MOUND. A Sect - FORT SASCATCHEWAN (2 guns) Relief was held up on account of severe hostile shelling of FORT HALIFAX.	CHW
		11.30 am	All guns registered with artillery and French Mortars	CHW

Army Form C. 2118.

WAR DIARY
or
INTELLIGENCE SUMMARY.
(Erase heading not required.)

Place	Date	Hour	Summary of Events and Information	Remarks and references to Appendices
			in extracting HITSCHEETE WOOD to an inline consecrated bombard- ment.	
		3.15p	Above was repeated. Enemy cease fire at Dukker.	
		3.45p	Retaliation on FORT HARRAS. There was one hole artillery hit. I round fuse 10.500.	
		11.30p	A practice barrage was carried out by attempt on divisional front. Much damage inflicted down to enemy trenches etc.	
			Casualties Captains NIL	
			Subalterns 3 OR to 92 M.G. Coy } Enter Company	
			1 OR to 33 do } Wienfelt	
			1 OR to 48 do	
			4 OR to 149 do	
			4 OR to 108 do	
			1 OR to OR (10 days leave)	Westley Lieut

Army Form C. 2118.

WAR DIARY
or
INTELLIGENCE SUMMARY.
(Erase heading not required.)

Place	Date	Hour	Summary of Events and Information	Remarks and references to Appendices
KLONDYKE Fm.	June 4th		During morning work on completion of 16 emplacements in the CHINESE WALL started. Cupola and sandbag shelter for Lewis gun were also made and stocked with S.A.A. Remainder of Company in reserve overhauled Lewis filling machines, guns, tripods etc. The was active throughout night firing on gaps in enemy wire and on C.T's. In rear of lines. Casualties. 2 O.R. to West. Camp.	O/R O/R
do	5th		Further preparations for the offensive carried out through out the day by working parties outside from H.Q. An advanced small station time fuse distributed South of ROSSIGNOL WOOD	Offm
	1630pm		A strong and successful raid was carried out by the 6th Connaught Rangers who entered enemy trenches	Offm Ognny

Army Form C. 2118.

Ref Sheet 28 SW 20/44

WAR DIARY
or
INTELLIGENCE SUMMARY.
(Erase heading not required.)

Instructions regarding War Diaries and Intelligence Summaries are contained in F. S. Regs., Part II. and the Staff Manual respectively. Title pages will be prepared in manuscript.

Place	Date	Hour	Summary of Events and Information	Remarks and references to Appendices
	June			
	1		In PETIT BOIS and advancing mit little opposition to MOAY SUPPORT TRENCH	
			Machine guns co-operated in the above and during the operation N°8 gun (THE HOUND) got a direct hit by an enemy shell & was put out of action. Night firing on customary targets as usual. Casualties 9	
			Arrival 2 officers 65 OR from various Battalions of the Brigade attached to act as carriers. Parties of the guard	O/h/M
			Stretcher B.R to C.C.S (2 sick 1 gassed)	
MESSINES F.M.	6		Final arrangements made for the offensive. The day passed with divisional artillery fire on the enemy lines.	
		9.30 pm	Coy from 6/L MIDDX FARM to take up battle positions YL O/MMM/00 guns in location holding the line circle north division	

Army Form C. 2118.

WAR DIARY
or
INTELLIGENCE SUMMARY.
(Erase heading not required.)

Place	Date	Hour	Summary of Events and Information	Remarks and references to Appendices
			and sent to their positions of assembly.	
			At 11.30 pm all guns were reported in position their distribution being as follows. Sections being allotted same roles as practised at YESTERDAY dummy training	
			2 guns A Section under Lt WILLIAMSON attached to 1st R MUNSTER FUSILIERS Assembly Point CHINESE WALL	
			2 " C " " Lt BLACKWELL " 6th R IRISH Regt Assembly Pt PARIS LINE	
			2 " D " " Lt WHITEHEAD " Lt LEINSTER Regt do	
			9 " (Composed of B Sect. and remaining subsections less 1 gun placed out of action on the 5th inst) mounted in the prepared emplacements in CHINESE WALL, under Lt WILSON.	
			This task allotted to guns were as follows:-	
			The guns of D & C Sections attached to LEINSTER Regt and R IRISH Regt to advance with the infantry, lifting guns on to objectives & the RED and BLUE LINES & consolidate the BLUE LINE	
			The 2 guns of A Sect to advance & take the R MUN MUNSTER FUS to consolidate the objective (the GREEN & BLACK LINES) and to consolidate the [signature]	

WAR DIARY
~~INTELLIGENCE SUMMARY~~
(Erase heading not required.)

Army Form C. 2118.

Place	Date	Hour	Summary of Events and Information	Remarks and references to Appendices
BLACK LINE			The nine guns on the CHINESE WALL to make a rolling barrage from ZERO onwards.	
			Objectives, boundaries and plan of barrage are shown on the accompanying map (Appendix A)	Appendix A
			Zero hour was 3.10 A.M. on morning of the 9th inst when mines were exploded along the whole front, and artillery opened fire.	
			As soon as the laying of the 9 in CHINESE WALL (notebook) had been checked (the explosions of the mines had rendered him forward laying inaccurate) all guns opened fire, and continued their barrage according to times shewn on Appendix B	Appendix B
			The 2 guns of Lieut WHITEHEAD with the assaulting Battalion left their normal terminal just after ZERO and reached their found objectives the BLUE LINE without trouble in opposition owing to the difficult ground and bad light, they lost direction slightly, this however was rectified and guns dug themselves in	

WAR DIARY
or
INTELLIGENCE SUMMARY.
(Erase heading not required.)

Army Form C. 2118.

Place	Date	Hour	Summary of Events and Information	Remarks and references to Appendices
			in at O19A67 and O19A56.	
			The two guns of Lt BLACKWELL then assembly according to programme but on account of then have crater formed by our own howitzers fallen in trying to rectify this Lt BLACKWELL was killed. Sergt SIMMONS however did recent work taking command of the guns regaining direction and finally consolidating in BLUE LINE at O19c51 and O19c59.	
			The two guns of Lt WILLIAMSON left their assembly locations in CHINESE WALLS with the 1st R MUNSTER FUSILIERS according to time-table and reached their final objective the BLACK LINE at 7.30AM and dug themselves in at O20c46.	
			Hostile artillery fire confined itself chiefly to the support trenches at the guns at CHINESE WALL two were put out of action (one permanently) by shellfire.	
			At 8.15 am the remaining seven guns left the CHINESE WALL and Offholm advancing in artillery formation reached WYTSCHAETE village at	2

WAR DIARY
INTELLIGENCE SUMMARY

Army Form C. 2118.

Place	Date	Hour	Summary of Events and Information	Remarks and references to Appendices
		8.30 AM	Position was taken up at 019089 guns having to move a little out of the bivouac area in order to get field of fire. S.A.A. and water were brought up to their gun position by pack mules and further by the carrying parties allotted to the Company from Battalion and a great deal was necessary on account of the intense heat. These guns supplied the guns in the BLACK LINE with S.A.A. etc while those in the BLUE LINE were outfitted by carrying parties from CHINESE WALL. During the afternoon the enemy shelled the BLACK & BLUE LINES heavily at intervals, and also throughout the night.	
			Casualties. 1 OR KILLED 3 OR wounded 1 OR Shellshock	
CHINESE WALL (Bde H.Q.)	June 8	11.30pm	On relief of Brigade the forward guns were withdrawn & placed in the BLUE LINE (leaving its garrison up to Brigade) and remainder placed in wood in CHINESE WALL. Casualties. KILLED 1 OR wounded 1 OR Shellshock 1 OR	
do	9th		On relief of Division by 11th Division guns were withdrawn from their positions	
			CHINESE WALL and BLUE LINE are the company marching back	

Army Form C. 2118.

WAR DIARY
or
INTELLIGENCE SUMMARY.
(Erase heading not required.)

Ref Sheet 28 SW

Place	Date	Hour	Summary of Events and Information	Remarks and references to Appendices
Mondite FM.	10th		Bn MONDITE FM. and bivy settled down by 1.30 AM (10th)	
			Day spent in cleaning up and resting, attached men returned to their Battalion.	Chs.
do	11th		Parades for cleaning of material kit etc	
			B.W. company were bathed at LOCRE	
			Casualtie. 1 O.R. to C.C.S. sick	Ch/s.
do	12th		Day spent in kit inspection and usual training (2 guns D Section mounted as anti-aircraft defence at CRUCIFIX CORNER M36/5 3T)	Ch/s.
			1 Off. to C.C.S. sick (2/Lt B.J. PHILLIPS.)	
do	13th		Company paraded at 8.30 AM marching order and marched to OUTTERSTEENE	
			Route taken — Cross country tracks to ST JANS CAPPEL — METEREN —	
			OUTTERSTEENE	
			2/Lt Lund of wound? — Coy called in billets.	
			Transfer but made marching hard + difficult	Ch/s.
Outtersteene	14th		Day spent in parades for cleaning up of material, personal etc	
			Casualties.	
			Arrival. 12 O.R. from BASE DEPOT.	Wholeon?

WAR DIARY
or
INTELLIGENCE SUMMARY
(Erase heading not required.)

Army Form C. 2118.

Place	Date	Hour	Summary of Events and Information	Remarks and references to Appendices
OUTTERSTEENE	June 15		Parade as follows :-	
		7am - 8am	Short route march, Physical Drill + Squad Drill	
		9.30am - 10.30	Gun Drill	
		10.30am - 11.30	" Shipping	
		11.30 - 12.30pm	Commanding Officers inspection of rifle during the parade the G.O.C. 16th Division also made an inspection of kits billets etc	
		2.30pm - 3pm	Rest filling competition.	
			Arrival. 1 Officer from Base Depot (2/Lt S.F. PETERS)	O/h/h/s
do	16th		Parade at the usual hour for Physical Drill, Route March, Bath, Gas helmet + Box respirator inspection + drill. Strength shown on AFD213 - 11 officers 192 OR	O/h/Casey MEF

Army Form C. 2118.

WAR DIARY
or
INTELLIGENCE SUMMARY
(Erase heading not required.)

Instructions regarding War Diaries and Intelligence Summaries are contained in F. S. Regs., Part II. and the Staff Manual respectively. Title pages will be prepared in manuscript.

Place	Date	Hour	Summary of Events and Information	Remarks and references to Appendices
OUTTERSTEENE	17th		Company moved to forward area.	
		4.30pm	Breakfasts	
		5.30am	Coy Parade	
		5.45	Coy marched off	
		9.40	Coy arrived at LOCRE and settled in DONCASTER HUTS. During the afternoon the DIEPENDAAL Sector of the line was reconnoitred in preparation of 18th Durham Light Infantry taking over Sector.	
		6.30pm	Relief other carried out.	CKhs.
LOCRE	18th		Company marched back to OUTTERSTEENE, taking over former billets. Time of departure 7.30 am. Time of arrival 11 am. Remainder of day was spent in testing & cleaning up of Equipment etc. 2 OR arrived from Base Rest Camp.	C/Walker Lieut

Army Form C. 2118.

WAR DIARY
or
INTELLIGENCE SUMMARY.
(Erase heading not required.)

(HAZEBROUCK Sheet 19
Sheet R.J. Sheet 27 (East))

Place	Date	Hour	Summary of Events and Information	Remarks and references to Appendices
OUTTERSTEENE	June 19th		Day spent in cleaning material of limbers, Lewis guns, equipment etc. and in inspections.	
			Casualties 1 O/R on leave to U.K. (10 days)	O/b.
	20th	5 am	Coy. moved to EECKE. Route followed OUTTERSTEENE - METEREN - FLETRE - THIEUSHOUT - EECKE. (R/ HAZEBROUCK MAP)	
		8.50 am	Time of arrival	
		2 pm	parade for cleaning of limbers etc	
		3 pm	foot inspection.	O/b.
			Casualties 1 O/R to C.C.S.	
EECKE	21st		Coy parade as follows :-	
		9.30 am	Company drill	
		10.30 am	Judging distance	
		11.30 am	Lecture	
		2 pm	foot inspection	
			Casualties Arrivals 8 O/R from BASE DEPOT	
			" 1 O/R from leave to U.K.	O/b.
			" 1 O/R to U.K. (10 day leave)	[signature] Lieut

Army Form C. 2118.

WAR DIARY
or
INTELLIGENCE SUMMARY.
(Erase heading not required.)

Instructions regarding War Diaries and Intelligence Summaries are contained in F. S. Regs., Part II. and the Staff Manual respectively. Title pages will be prepared in manuscript.

Map Ref. S Sheet 27
Sheet 19.

Place	Date	Hour	Summary of Events and Information	Remarks and references to Appendices
EECKE	22nd	4 AM	Company paraded to march to ZEGGERS - CAPPEL Area. Route taken EECKE - STEENVOORDE - WORMHOUDT - ESQUELBECQ - X Roads B.6.2.a. (Sheet 27) - SPREEW - tot - T.23.c.27 (Sheet 19).	
		9 up to Hour of arrival.	Rain fell heavily during whole of the march and on reaching billets attempts were made to dry the clothing of the men.	O.K.S.
F^me LOYSKNOCKE	23rd	9.30 AM } 12.30 PM }	Cleaning of billets & contents.	
		2-3 PM	Foot Inspection.	
			Casualties	
			1 off + 8 o.r. struck off strength having been evacuated but no official information being received	
			Off Strength Officers 18 / O.R.	Ch. Wilson /r.

Army Form C. 2118.

WAR DIARY
or
INTELLIGENCE SUMMARY.
(Erase heading not required.)

Instructions regarding War Diaries and Intelligence Summaries are contained in F. S. Regs., Part II. and the Staff Manual respectively. Title pages will be prepared in manuscript.

Place	Date	Hour	Summary of Events and Information	Remarks and references to Appendices
Ft LITHICK	24th to 26th		Spent in Company training in the following subjects:- Physical drill (daily) Route Marching Gun Drill Saluting drill Company drill Map reading for N.C.O.s Semaphore signalling Barr & Stroud Rangefinder. Inspection of kit, hut & loose also took place	
			Casualties (struck off strength	
	26th		1 O.R. Sick	
	25th		Arrivals 2nd Lt R.J. WEBB } from BASE DEPOT. 2nd Lt W.E. WALLACE	Chateauroux
			OTHER DEPARTURES (not affecting strength) 24th 1 O.R. to A.P.M. (to undergo sentence) 25th 1 O.R. to U.K. (10 days leave)	to F.P.N.1

WAR DIARY or INTELLIGENCE SUMMARY

Army Form C. 2118.

Place	Date	Hour	Summary of Events and Information	Remarks and references to Appendices
Fn Lorrier	27th	9.30 a.m.	Inspection of the Coy whilst on the march by D.O.C. XIXth Corps	
		1.15 p	Coy parade in drill order	
		1.30	C.O.'s inspection (Stores?)	
		1.45	Coy marched to B9C 91 and marched Coy	
		12.30 H	Coy returned to billets	
		2-3 pm	Belt filling by hand	
			Temperature (not affecting strength) 2 O.R. to No 21 Squadron R.F.C. on anti-aircraft duties	Ch W
			Company training carried on in Lewis drive, stripping of stoppage mechanism Aeroplane Gun drill combining Lewis gun making use of natural features of the ground, unit marching under level drive squad drill Lectures etc	
			Casualties 2 OR struck off strength 2 ot	
	28th			
	29th		Departures (not affecting strength) 29th 1 off Clark to U.K. (10 days) (Capt Clapham	Oj Gleam
	30th		30th 1 off Course at 21 Squadron R.F.C. (2nd Lt R J Nebb)	
			admitted C.C.S. (sick) (Lt A.R Williamson)	

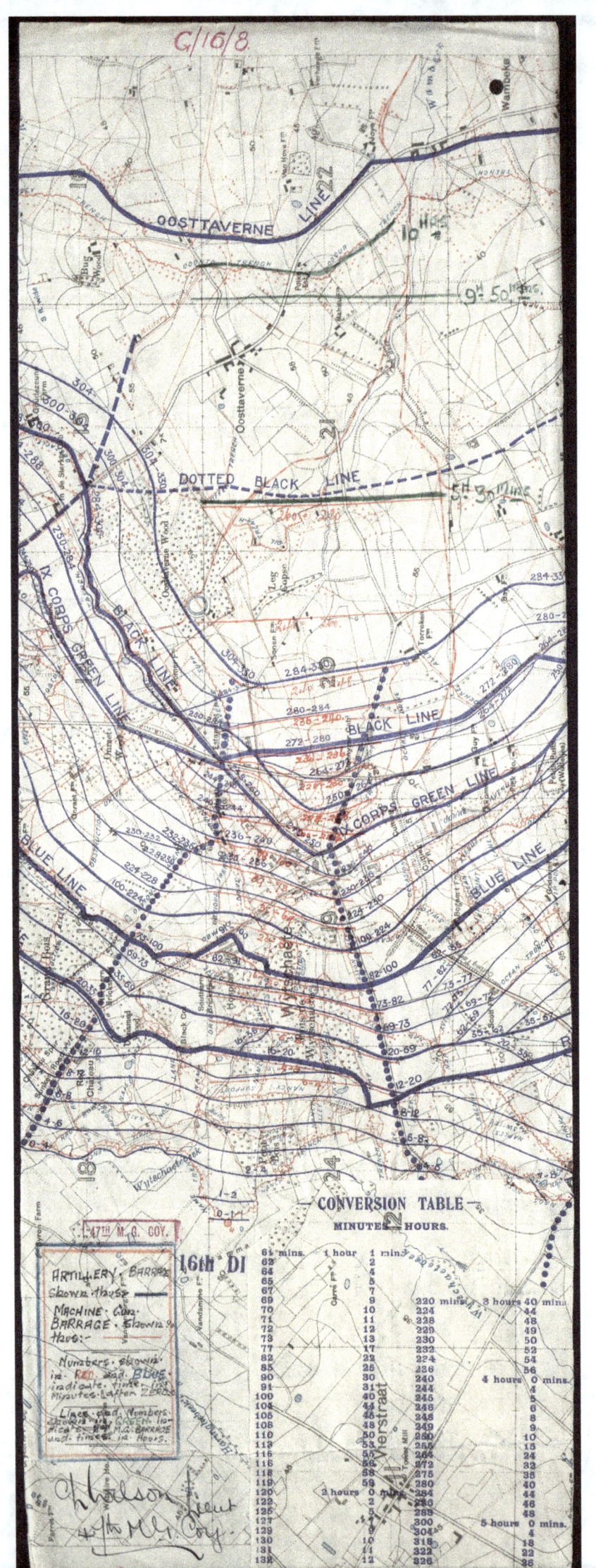

47th M.G. Coy

APPENDIX 1.

WAR DIARY
JUNE 1917.

WAR DIARY.

FOR MONTH OF JULY, 1917.

VOLUME :- 16

UNIT :- 47th Machine Gun Coy.
M.G.C.

WAR DIARY
or
INTELLIGENCE SUMMARY.
(Erase heading not required.)

Army Form C. 2118.

Place	Date	Hour	Summary of Events and Information	Remarks and references to Appendices
LEGGERS-CAPPEL AREA	July 1st		Training carried out in ordinary M.G. subjects and in attack and Barrage tire Practices.	
			Bursts inspected on two occasions by G.O.C. 47th Inf Bde	
	11th		On the 11th not a Competition was held in T.E.T. and action judged by the G.O.C.	
			The following arrived & departures not affecting strength took place.	
			1st Officer from leave to U.K.	
			2nd Officer & 3 O.R. to G.H.Q. Omega Arms School on course	
			3rd Officer to 21st Squadron R.F.C. on Anti Aircraft Course	
			1 O.R. from leave to U.K.	
			1 Officer 21st Squad R.F.C.	
			6th 1 Officer from 21 Squad R.F.C.	
			1 O.R. do do	
			1 Officer & 3 O.R. to 5th Army Test Camp	
			1st Company Strength on AFB213 11 off 184 O.R.	Wilson
				1/C

Army Form C. 2118.

WAR DIARY
or
INTELLIGENCE SUMMARY.
(Erase heading not required.)

Instructions regarding War Diaries and Intelligence Summaries are contained in F.S. Regs., Part II. and the Staff Manual respectively. Title pages will be prepared in manuscript.

Place	Date	Hour	Summary of Events and Information	Remarks and references to Appendices
ZEGGERS-CAPPEL AREA	Sep		Casualties not attending divine service (see annex)	
	5th		On 5th R. from leave to UK	
	6th		On 9th 5th from 9th Squadron HC	
			1st do	
	10th		1st do	
	11th		1st from leave	
			1st from leave	
	12th		The Company paraded at 8am and marched to WINNEZEELE and were billeted in No 2 Area.	
			Men & arrival 11th H.	
			Remained 1 day spent in cleaning huts etc.	
	13th		The Coy paraded at 9am & marched to BRANDHOEK Route:— WATOU — POPERINGHE — BRANDHOEK	
			Arrived at 11.30am & Co established in Camp #34 6/1/16 M/W	
			Coy detailed to 5th Division for future instruction.	

WAR DIARY or INTELLIGENCE SUMMARY

Army Form C. 2118.

Place	Date	Hour	Summary of Events and Information	Remarks and references to Appendices
BRANDHOEK			Casualties 1 O.R. to stop IP	
	14		Strength of Bn	
			Casualties O.R. 2/Lt T.J. SHAFFIELD joined the Bn from new Sectn Trenches. Strength on 23 Officers 182 o.r.	
	17th		Troops absence (with Co) succeeded by Lambets for church party of 3 offrs & 100 OR attended to new MENIN GATE YPRES. Later attempt at HAYMARKET carried material to Little about crater in dug out lines were taken up by carrying Party returned to HQ at 5am. 2 guns of D Coy & 1 OC det under 2/Lt HERR and 2/Lt HEBB relieved 2 guns of A H5th Coy (6th Aust Div) in one team were taken in lorry to blair Erksdale	

Army Form C. 2118.

WAR DIARY
or
INTELLIGENCE SUMMARY.
(Erase heading not required.)

Instructions regarding War Diaries and Intelligence Summaries are contained in F. S. Regs. Part II. and the Staff Manual respectively. Title pages will be prepared in manuscript.

Place	Date	Hour	Summary of Events and Information	Remarks and references to Appendices
			(2 O.R. wounded etc	D.L.
			Casualties 1 O.R. to UK (10 days leave)	
BRANDHOEK.	July 16th		Seven enemy shelling reported from town by day and a gas-shell attack during the night. Many shells fallen around the SCHOOL-HOUSE, YPRES. HAYMARKET, PICCADILLY & HALF-MOON TRENCH during days sections at H.Q. practised barrage-fire. did usual working parties. Working party of 2 offs & 111 sent to Canadies	
			took in (?)	O/C
			1 O.R. evacuated sick.	
	17th		Parades as usual for sections at H.Q. Heavy shelling by the enemy affected our line but the intensity of the bombardment of yesterday was not felt. 2 offs + 110 OR proceeded to HAYMARKET	W. Nelson
			Sgt Nosting(?) party of 2 off + 110 OR proceeded to HAYMARKET	

WAR DIARY
or
INTELLIGENCE SUMMARY
(Erase heading not required.)

Army Form C. 2118.

Place	Date	Hour	Summary of Events and Information	Remarks and references to Appendices
BRANDHOEK	July		to carry on work on battery positions	
	(continued)		2 teams B Section + 1 team A Section relieved teams of C.D at 11.45PM Lieut Dixon returned 2/Lt MERRY en Section H.Q in St JAMES TRENCH and 2/Lt PETERS relieving 2/Lt WEBB in SCHOOL HOUSE. Relief was carried out without mishap in spite of shelling of YPRES + all communication trenches the relieved teams were utilized in carrying parties in addition to the working party. Both parties returned at daylight + arrived at H.Q at 5.15 A.M	Chs.
	18th		Parades + working parties as usual more work was able to be done as the enemy artillery confined his energies to back areas chiefly	C/Ibbotson/.

WAR DIARY
or
INTELLIGENCE SUMMARY

Army Form C. 2118.

Place	Date	Hour	Summary of Events and Information	Remarks and references to Appendices
BRANDHOEK	July 19th		Maind H.G. parade by sections at H.Q. Fairly quiet apart from lieu during day	
		8pm	Working party of 2 offs + 40 OR proceeded to trenches but (two teams of C₁ Sect. + one of B) under 2/Lt WEBB. These teams relieved the teams of A + B Sections. The enemy showed a severe barrage of gas + HE shell on communication trenches etc + great difficulty was experienced in getting up S.A.A. + material which had to be dumped at various points. Casualties. 4 O.R. wounded (1 remaining at duty)	
			The following awards were made for honours services rendered during the MESSINES operations	
			CAPTAIN J.W. CLAPHAM Military Cross	
			C.S.M. HUMPHRIES D.C.M.	
			SERT SIMMONS D.C.M.	Chulsen

Army Form C. 2118.

WAR DIARY
or
INTELLIGENCE SUMMARY.
(Erase heading not required.)

Instructions regarding War Diaries and Intelligence Summaries are contained in F. S. Regs., Part II. and the Staff Manual respectively. Title pages will be prepared in manuscript.

Place	Date	Hour	Summary of Events and Information	Remarks and references to Appendices
BRANDHOEK	July 20	A.M.	Parades for men at H.Q. as follows	
		7.30-8	Physical Drill	
		9.30-10.30	Gun Drill	
		10.30-11.30	Stripping	
		11.30-12.30pm	Cleaning of guns, spare parts &c.	
		2-3pm	Semaphore Signalling	
			Heavy shelling of HAYMARKET & ST JAMES TRENCH reported from line.	
		2pm	Working party of 1 off & 20 O.R. proceeded to School House	
		8pm	" " " " " to work on HAYMARKET	
			position. The former party who remain for 24 hrs at School House, worked on position in PICCADILLY SWITCH	
			Casualties.	
			1 O.R. Killed in Action } SHELL FIRE.	
			2 O.R. Wounded }	O/C Batln

Army Form C. 2118.

WAR DIARY
or
INTELLIGENCE SUMMARY.
(Erase heading not required.)

Place	Date	Hour	Summary of Events and Information	Remarks and references to Appendices
BRANDHOEK	July 21st		Parade as usual for men at H.Q. Shortly on left firing.	
			Cleaning S.A.A.	
			Working party at the School Ho. engaged on emptying S.A.A. + R.E. material to dump/ration.	
		9. Before 3 guns in turn relieved by Ant. Cay - 46th Coy. Relief complete by 12 mn when the teams returned to H.Q. during enemy gas shell bombardment.		
		4 P.M. A working party of 2 NCOs & 2 aiR under 2/Lt MEARY relieved the working party under 2/Lt PETERS at School House.		
			Bad dear bottle went astray took up line during the night the relieved teams returning to HQ at 5AM	O/L
			Strength of Coy down to AFB 213. 10 officers 171 O.R.	
	22d		Church Parade, cleaning up of camp etc & general fatigues for men at H.Q.	
			Working party at School House carried on as usual	A/Wilson
			Casualties BASE (Pte HAMMETT) inefficient	

Army Form C. 2118.

WAR DIARY
or
INTELLIGENCE SUMMARY.
(Erase heading not required.)

Instructions regarding War Diaries and Intelligence Summaries are contained in F. S. Regs., Part II. and the Staff Manual respectively. Title pages will be prepared in manuscript.

Place	Date	Hour	Summary of Events and Information	Remarks and references to Appendices
BRAMSHOTT	May 23rd		Parade as usual for sections at H.Q.	
		4pm	1st SHEFFIELD & 22nd Relieved 1st MERRY & working part at School Ho.	
			Both parties were engaged in carrying etc throughout the night and relieved parties returned to H.Q. at	
			3am having to pass through a dense challe gas	Ohh
		2/L	attack	
			School at H.Q. utilised for cleaning & examining all L.A.A. and filling belts. Limbed backed with Belt Boxes, ready to transporting to trenches at night.	
		7.45pm	Working party of 20/S. and two OR's. proceeded to trenches.	/S
			L.A.A. & ammn. from Ammunition Dump, and thus -	
			together with Belt Boxes were carried to Battery Position	
			in ST. JAMES' TRENCH and stored in DUG-OUTS and RECESSES	
			adjoining positions.	
			Comparatively quiet night the enemy paying no real attention to Back Areas.	

J.S. Saffield /S

WAR DIARY
INTELLIGENCE SUMMARY

Army Form C. 2118.

Place	Date	Hour	Summary of Events and Information	Remarks and references to Appendices
BRANDHOEK			CASUALTIES:- Strength Increase:- 1 O.R. from Base Depot.	
	28th	9.30 a.m.	The Band at H.Q. paraded for usual M.G. training	
		12.30 p.m.	Owing morning	
		7.15 p.m.	Working party consisting of 2 Offs. and 40 ORs. proceeded to trenches and completed work on battery position in ST. JAMES' TRENCH. Enemy hostile shelling with CWs shells.	
			※ Lt. C.L. WILSON slightly wounded whilst inspecting battery position.	
			Lt. J. SWAFFIELD and working party relieved at SCHOOL HOUSE by a M.G. Coy. of 18th Division.	
			※ CASUALTIES - 1 officer wounded.	

JL Batfield Lt.

WAR DIARY
or
INTELLIGENCE SUMMARY.

Army Form C. 2118.

Place	Date	Hour	Summary of Events and Information	Remarks and references to Appendices
BRANDHOEK	20th	—	Lt. J. SWAFFIELD assumes temporary Command of Company.	
	26th		Company training on following subjects:-	
			Practice Damage Fire.	
			Use of Obstruction Stops.	
			Gun Drill.	
			Mechanism.	
			Immediate Action.	
			Belt filling - Hand and Machine.	
	28th		CASUALTIES:-	
			2 O.R. from line to Dépôt.	
	29th		1 Off. + 3 O.R. from Course at G.H.Q. Small Arms School.	
			2 O.R. returned from St Omer Rest Camp.	

J.Swaffield/Lt

Army Form C. 2118.

WAR DIARY
or
INTELLIGENCE SUMMARY.
(Erase heading not required.)

Instructions regarding War Diaries and Intelligence Summaries are contained in F. S. Regs., Part II. and the Staff Manual respectively. Title pages will be prepared in manuscript.

Place	Date	Hour	Summary of Events and Information	Remarks and references to Appendices
BRANDHOEK	July 29th	—	Divine Service. Company tasks until night.	
		9:00 pm	Guns and limbers and teams for dump sent to SCHOOL HOUSE.	
			CASUALTIES. — NIL.	f.
	30th		Final preparations made for the attack.	
		10:00pm	Bombard proceeded to trenches and occupied positions allotted for barrage line Jackcoat.	f.
	31st		"All Guns in position and all correct" was reported to H.Q. at 3.20 am.	

J. Satsfield L[?]

Army Form C. 2118.

WAR DIARY
or
INTELLIGENCE SUMMARY.
(Erase heading not required.)

Place	Date	Hour	Summary of Events and Information	Remarks and references to Appendices
TRENCHES	31st	3.50. a.m.	"A" and "B" Batteries opened fire (maximum rate) on targets shown on Appendix "B".	attached
			The Organization Orders showing Position of Batteries, Targets, Time of Lifts, Rate of fire and instructions extent of "F.O.O's" are shown in Appendix "B".	attached
			Lines of movement and additions of armoured Batteries after first shoot are shown in Appendix "B".	attached
			The attack was carried out in stages, bright and fine.	
			Phases:—	
			1st Objectives:— Enemy's front line, Eastern of Zevekot to Pine (this inland was from 200 yds to 500 yds before the 2nd Objectives; Enemy's Reserve Line, it is intended up and consolidating the BLACK LINE (which East of the PINE LINE) 16 and including the BLACK LINE (which east of the PINE LINE (BLUE LINE) line was advanced to this line as advanced at this the advance was 20 round after ZERO	

Staff/WCS

Army Form C. 2118.

WAR DIARY
or
INTELLIGENCE SUMMARY.
(Erase heading not required.)

Instructions regarding War Diaries and Intelligence Summaries are contained in F. S. Regs., Part II. and the Staff Manual respectively. Title pages will be prepared in manuscript.

Place	Date	Hour	Summary of Events and Information	Remarks and references to Appendices
TRENCHES	31st		3rd Objective. The attack was continued at Zero + 6hr. 20 mins (10:00 am) on the Frontage 3rd Inns Lufsion (THE LANDMARK — GHEULVELT LINE) into K and instructing the GREEN LINE which is from 150x to 300x East of the BLACK LINE. Owing to the whole being of the attack all 6 Guns (moved up to 2 Batteries) and 1 "C" Battery in EAST LANE, HALF MOON and HAYMARKET TRENCHES. 1 "B" Battery in DULY SWITCH contained to the Artillery barrage according to programme, and effects at times later in abeyance to. When the 3rd objective has been gained attacking barrage was put down in advance of the GREEN LINE — Limation — known. The Barrage programme then came to an end. "B" and "C" Batteries commenced reports on defilated "A" and "D" Batteries — Machen and are marked at advanced "A" and "D" Batteries.	

J. Haffnell Lt

Army Form C. 2118.

WAR DIARY
or
INTELLIGENCE SUMMARY.
(Erase heading not required.)

Instructions regarding War Diaries and Intelligence Summaries are contained in F. S. Regs., Part II. and the Staff Manual respectively. Title pages will be prepared in manuscript.

Place	Date	Hour	Summary of Events and Information	Remarks and references to Appendices
MENIN GATE	July 31st	—	Total casualties to 12 midnight :- 2 O.R. Killed. 15 O.R. Wounded.	J Chappell /s

APPENDIX "F".

PROGRAMME OF MOVES.

Division.	Battery.	Moves.	Remarks.
15th	B1.	Advance to B2 at Zero + 6 hrs. 50 mins. Move to be completed by Zero + 7 hrs. 32 mins.	
	C1.	Advance to C2 at Zero + 6 hrs. 50 mins. Move to be completed by Zero + 7 hrs. 32 mins.	

APPENDIX "B"

M.G. fire organization Roster.

No. of group Battery	No. of guns	Formation	Location	Swing from – to	Target	Rate of fire	Remarks
B	2	H/4 M.G. Coy.	I.11.a.24.74.	0 – 18	I.6.b.53.53. To C.30.d.11.21.	1 belt per ½ min	Search 1700 yds beyond target. Dispersion shifts to be set for A.F. of target.
				19 – 15.	D.25.c.90.90. To D.25.a.60.10	½ belt per ½ min.	Search 200 yds beyond target. Dispersion shifts to be set for A.F. of target. On S.O.S. after maximum rate of fire on target for 10 mins. Continue at ordinary rate of fire also.
B.1	2	H. M.G. Coy.	I.6.b.58.85.	16.1.93.	D.25.d.11.58. To D.27.a.69.25.	1 belt per ½ min	Dispersion shifts to be set for A.F. of target.
				6.08. 6.32.	D.25.a.76.57. To D.20.c.60.35.		Hostile barrage as on formation. On S.O.S. fire maximum rate of fire for 10 min & continue ordinary rate of fire for 5 mins.
				6.33. 6.50.	D.25.a.76.57. To D.20.c.60.35.	1 belt per 4 min.	Search 300 yds beyond target. Dispersion shifts to be set for A.F. of target.
					D.20.d.65.02. To I.25.a.50.80	1 belt per 4 min.	Search 300 yds beyond target. Dispersion shifts to be set for A.F. of target.
B.2	2	H/ M.G. Coy.	D.25.c.95.65.	7.32. 8.c.	D.21.c.37.08. To D.21.6.08.87.	1 belt per ½ min.	Search 200 yds beyond target. Dispersion shifts to be set for A.F. of target. On S.O.S. maximum rate of fire to be opened on target & continue for 10 mins. & then continue at ordinary rate of fire for 5 mins.

APPENDIX "B"

M.G. Fire Organization Order.

Group or Batt.	No. of Guns	Location	Timing From / To	Target	Rate of fire	Remarks
C	8	At M.G. Coy.	I.5.c.13.13.	0. 18.	C.30.d. 56.90 To C.30.a. 94.08.	Not pour 4 rounds.	Search 400 yds beyond target. Depression stops to be set for R.E. of target.
			19. 15	D.25.a. 90.00. To D.25.a. 15.59.	1 belt per 4 guns.	Search 400 yds beyond target. Depression stops to be set for R.E. of target. On S.O.S. maximum rate of fire for 10 mins on target & continue at ordinary rate & after.
			9.6. 9.33.	D.25.b. 15.77. To D.25.b. 65.17.	1600 rds per 4 guns.	Depression stops to be set for R.E. of target.
C.1	2	At M.G. Coy.	C.30.d. 32.80.		D.20.c.71.92. To D.20.a. 31.11.	Fire one belt as soon as in position. On S.O.S. open maximum rate of fire for 10 mins and continue ordinary rate of fire for 5 mins.
			6.08-6.38.	D.20.c.71.92. To D.20.a. 31.11.	14 belts per 2 guns.	Search 300 yds beyond target. Depression stops to be set for R.E. of target.
			6.33 650	D.20.d. 50.60.15 D.20.c. 22.56.	1 belt per 2 guns.	Search 300 yds beyond target. Depression stops to be set for R.E. of target.
C.2	8	At M.G. Coy.	D.25.a. 30.35	7.52 9.20.	D.21.b.85.87 To D.18.b.88.60.	1 belt per gun.	Search 500 yds beyond target. Depression stops to be set for level target. On S.O.S. maximum rate of fire to be opened on target & continue for 10 mins & then continue at ordinary rate for 5 mins.

WAR DIARY.

FOR MONTH OF AUGUST, 1917.

VOLUME ...17...

UNIT 4Y.B. Machine Gun Coy.

No 47 Machine Gun Company.

War Diary
- for -
August.
- 1917 -

Army Form C. 2118.

WAR DIARY
or
INTELLIGENCE SUMMARY.
(Erase heading not required.)

Place	Date	Hour	Summary of Events and Information	Remarks and references to Appendices
TRENCHES	1-8-17		Company in the line with 15th Div occupying breastworks in POTINZE DEFENCES & SCHOOL HOUSE. Casualties 1 wounded, 1 missing	
BRANDHOEK AREA	2-8-17		Company came out of Line & returned to Camp arriving at 8 p.m.	
"	3-8-17		Parade 9.30 a.m. to 12.30 p.m. General Cleaning up of Gen. Equipment. Company rested for the remainder of the day.	
"	4-8-17		Parade 9.30 Limber Cleaning & Co. Training & Machine Gunner from Base Arrival	

J. Chatfield, Lt.

Army Form C. 2118.

WAR DIARY
or
INTELLIGENCE SUMMARY.
(Erase heading not required.)

Instructions regarding War Diaries and Intelligence Summaries are contained in F.S. Regs., Part II. and the Staff Manual respectively. Title pages will be prepared in manuscript.

Place	Date	Hour	Summary of Events and Information	Remarks and references to Appendices
BRANDHOEK AREA	5-8-17		Parade. 7-30 to 8.00 Physical Drill	
		9.30 " 10.30	General Action	
		10.30 " 12.30	Bell filling by Lance & Maclean	J.L.
			2/Lieuts. 2 Maclean Joined from leave	
ST LAWRENCE CAMP	6-8-17		Parade. 8.00 a.m. Move to St LAWRENCE CAMP	J.L.
			Departure 2 Maclean Joined to line	
"	7-8-17		Parade. 7.30 to 8.00 Physical Drill	
		9.30 " 12.30	Inspection of Iron Ration identity Discs etc	
"	8-8-17		Parade. 7.30 to 8.00 Physical Drill	
		10.30 " 11.30	Bell filling by Tank	
		11.30 " 12.30	Cleaning Guns	
			Captain R.C. Maud assumed duty as C.O. Unaffected.	

Army Form C. 2118.

WAR DIARY
or
INTELLIGENCE SUMMARY.
(Erase heading not required.)

Place	Date	Hour	Summary of Events and Information	Remarks and references to Appendices
N° LAWRENCE CAMP	8-9-17		2 Lt J.A. Bagclift from Base Depot. 1 O.R. from Corps Reinforcement Camp	ft
"	9-9-17		Parade 9-30 a.m. Commanding Officers Inspection. Lieut E.T. Leeborough from 46 M.G. Coy. 1 Ofr. 30 O.R. from Royal Munster Fus. attached to Coy for Field Operations.	ft
"	10-9-17		Co parade. Batt. proceed to Trenches to Look at "Emplacements". 3 O.R. Killed. 2 O.R. wounded. Arrived 15 Machine Gunners from 16 Div Depot. Departure Lieut Smith to 196 M.G. Coy.	ft

J Bartfield Lt

Army Form C. 2118.

WAR DIARY
or
INTELLIGENCE SUMMARY.
(Erase heading not required.)

Place	Date	Hour	Summary of Events and Information	Remarks and references to Appendices
ST LAWRENCE CAMP	11-8-17		Divine Service Annual 4 O.R. from camp Departure 3 O.R. on leave 2 O.R. to C.C.S.	A.
"	12-8-17		Parade 7-30 & 8.0. Physical drill 9-30 - 12.30 Gun cleaning, I.A. o Gun drill Departure 2/Lt R.A. Wagstaff to 30 Gen Hospital	
"	13-8-17		Parades 7.8.0 & 8.0 Physical drill 9-30 - 12.30 Battery gun drill	A.
"	14-8-17		Preparation made for sending A & B Section away to line with 8 Group.	

Wagstaff Lt

Army Form C. 2118.

WAR DIARY
or
INTELLIGENCE SUMMARY.
(Erase heading not required.)

Place	Date	Hour	Summary of Events and Information	Remarks and references to Appendices
VLAMERTINGHE AREA	15-8-17		Newport moved to new Camp at Clauwetinghem during C.O's Scheme left for Brenton Rearmement of Coy moving to Camp at Clauwetinghe at 6.30 P.M. 2 Lt R.J. Lebbi attached to 48 M.G. Coy for Active Operation. 2 O.R. sent to U.K.	
	16-8-17		See Operation Orders. Casualties. 6 O.R. Killed 21 " Wounded 1 " Missing	2 Lt W.E. WALLACE Wounded Missing Recovered at duty.

Army Form C. 2118.

WAR DIARY
or
INTELLIGENCE SUMMARY.
(Erase heading not required.)

Place	Date	Hour	Summary of Events and Information	Remarks and references to Appendices
TRENCHES	17-8-17		Company in the line Croallü	
			Regt. Orders No 12/1/18 Coy evacuated position in the line & relieved by Camp at Beaufort Lines Rawlinge at 3.00 am	
VLAMERTINGHE AREA	18-8-17		Troops bathed all morning & afternoon. 8.0 p.m. All ranks packed ready to move & baths	
WATOU AREA	19-8-17		Company parade at 6.45 am. Moved for war off 7.0am Arrived at Camp at Watou B.13.d.34 at 10.15am	

J.H. Offield Lt

Army Form C. 2118.

WAR DIARY
or
INTELLIGENCE SUMMARY.
(Erase heading not required.)

Place	Date	Hour	Summary of Events and Information	Remarks and references to Appendices
WATOU AREA	19.8.17		General cleaning up of equipment &c. Company holding Parade 1530. O.R. from Base Depot	ft.
"	20.8.17		Packing limbers & preparing for route march to use. Coy. 1.30 p.m. Coy moves off.	
			Coy marched to EECKE Area via CAËSTRE Coy arrives at 5.30 p.m. H.Q. established at Q.7.b.9.6. O/c Coy Billeted Bullis at 5.45 p.m.	ft.
EECKE	21.8.17		Preparation for further Route march. Moved off at 2.30 p.m. Marched to CAËSTRE & entrained for SOMME front. Arrived 3.5 O.R. from Base depot.	ft.
BAPAUME	22.8.17		Arrived at 2.30 a.m. marched to Y.M.C.A. Hut & Company billeted with light refreshments & rest until dawn.	
			Coy then marched via BIEFVILLERS - BIHUCOURT - ad ACHIET-LE-GRAND & GOMMECOURT	J Gaffney Lt

Army Form C. 2118.

WAR DIARY
or
INTELLIGENCE SUMMARY.
(Erase heading not required.)

Instructions regarding War Diaries and Intelligence Summaries are contained in F. S. Regs., Part II. and the Staff Manual respectively. Title pages will be prepared in manuscript.

Place	Date	Hour	Summary of Events and Information	Remarks and references to Appendices
GOMMIE COURT	22.8.17		Adv HQ well established in Camp N of village	
"	23.8.17		Company parade. Usual training in M.G. subjects	
"	24.8.17		parade 9.30 to 10.30 Gen Drill 10.30 - 11.30 Mechanism 11.30 - 12.30 Semaphore Action	
"	25.8.17		Preparation made for taking over sector in BULLECOURT sector	
"	25.8.17 2.30pm		Section marched to Gorand Aera via ERVILLERS-ST LEGER Transport moves to N. of line of ERVILLERS Section relieved 62 & 64 M.G. Cops the line as for attacked operation orders. HQ established at T.30.a.11 at 5.30 p.m.	J Shaffell L.

Army Form C. 2118.

WAR DIARY
or
INTELLIGENCE SUMMARY.
(Erase heading not required.)

Place	Date	Hour	Summary of Events and Information	Remarks and references to Appendices
TRENCHES	26.8.17		Relief reported complete at 6.15 a.m.	
	28.8.17		No incident for about 24 hours. Employments, dugouts & trenches leading to believe worked on throughout. Enemy put usual attention to Tank System of Trenches, but Willway & Mackies Guns in the Shell hole area for quite Sniper active.	
TRENCHES	29.8.17		Quiet during day. Information having been obtained from a prisoner that an enemy relief would be in progress at night, guns opened on targets as follows—	
			R1 3. SUNKEN ROAD — 1000 rounds	
			RT 4 TRIDENT ALLEY 720 "	
			RT 6 FAG ALLEY 900 "	
			Re-circulation by L.MG M.G. has been	

J Chatfield /L

WAR DIARY
or
INTELLIGENCE SUMMARY

(Erase heading not required.)

Army Form C. 2118.

Hour, Date, Place	Summary of Events and Information	Remarks and references to Appendices
TRENCHES. 30.8.17	So much firing. Artillery normal April from line. Germans reinforced the necessary & building of "dug-outs" & labour commenced at General position. Enemy Artillery activity on the front Attacks paid to back Arran hill day	
31.8.17		

J.S. Hughes/7

No 47. M.G. Coy.
Operation Order No 1.

Copy No 1

Map. Ref.
PREZENBERG:
1:10,000.

15th Augt. 1917.

1) Action of M.G. Coy.

There will be 4 batteries of 4 guns each at C.D.E.&G. as per attached map.

These guns will fire on barrage lines as given on attached map.

2) Lifts.

Following is table of lifts for guns.

Barrage No 1. Zero to Zero + 8. Rate of fire 250 rounds per 2 minutes. Search to 400 yds beyond target. Traverse as laid down.

Barrage No 2. Zero +9 to Zero +35. Same rate of fire and depth of search.

Barrage No 3. Zero +36 to Zero +120. Rate of fire - 250 rounds per 4 minutes, until Zero + 120 after which it will be maintained at the rate of 250 rounds per 15 minutes until Zero +150 when it will cease.   No 3 is the PROTECTIVE barrage line and it is most important that guns must at all times be prepared to open a protective barrage on it.

On ceasing fire one gun per battery at a time is to be cleaned, have new barrel put in and tested.

3. On capture of RED DOTTED LINE Officers i/ch D & G. batteries will either proceed themselves or send responsible N.C.O. to reconnoitre for positions at the following places.

BORRY FARM   D. 25. B.   2 guns   D. battery
VAMPIR   D. 26. A   2 -   G   -

The approximate positions of the above are shown on map supplied to Officers concerned. These positions will be occupied by guns brought forward from the original barrage positions as soon as the situation permits.

On reaching their new positions these guns will lay on Protective Barrage line No 3. They will arrange to bring S.A.A. from their original positions.

4. S.A.A. Every man will carry at least two bandoliers of S.A.A. Those who are not carrying other gun material will carry four bandoliers. On arrival in the line these bandoliers will be stacked carefully at the gun positions.
Details of dumps of S.A.A. have been given to officers concerned.
Oil in petrol cans will be taken up by sections.

5. S.O.S.   Green Very lights.

6. Coy Hdqs. at Mill Cott (C.S.A. 18.) Hdqs of 49th Inf. Bde. as soon as guns are in position, which must be by 1 hour before Zero notification will be sent to Coy. Hdqs. by runner.

7. Zero.   Hour will be notified later.

[signature] Captain.
Commanding
No. 147 M.G. Coy.

Issued to:-
1 & 2. War Diary
3. File
4 O.C. A Sections
5 — B "
6 — C "
7 — D "
8 A.M.G.O.

47th M.G. Company OPERATION ORDER. No. 103.

Copy No. 1.

Ref. Maps. Sheet. 51ᴮ and 57ᶜ   25th Aug. 1917.

1. THE following relief will take place to-day:—

(a) Three Sections (A, C, and D) of No. 47 M.G. Coy. will relieve Three sections of No. 64 M.G. Coy.

(b) One Section (B) of No. 47 M.G. Coy will relieve one Section of No. 62 M.G. Coy.

SECTIONS will relieve as follows:—

"A" Section will occupy positions:—
R.F. 1. } under Lt. QUALTROUGH.
R.F. 2. } under Lt. WILLIAMSON } will relieve Lt. BUCKLE.
R.S. 6. }
R.S. 7. }

"C" Section will occupy positions:—
R.I. 1. } under Lt. WHITEHEAD and 2/Lt. WEBB, will relieve
R.I. 2. } Lt. BARROW.
R.S. 1. }
R.S. 2. }

"D" Section will occupy positions:—
R.S. 3. } under Lt. QUALTROUGH. will relieve Lt. FITTER.
R.S. 4. }
R.S. 5. } under 2/Lt. MERRY. will relieve Lt. TOLLER.
R.S. 8. }

"B" Section will occupy positions:—
R.I. 3. }
R.I. 4. } under 2/Lt. WALLACE and 2/Lt. PETERS.
R.I. 5. }
R.I. 6. }

2. Sections will take up Guns, Tripods, etc, and 8 Belt Boxes per gun. The Company will march through ERVILLERS and ST. LEGER to CROISILLES CHURCH where guides will be at 4:00.p.m. Sections will move at intervals of 15 minutes.
Inventories of all maps, charts, S.O.S. lines, work on hand and work to be done will be taken and signed. Lists of trench stores will be taken in duplicate.
Completion of relief to be reported to Company H.Q.
Company H.Q. will be at T.30.a.1.1.

3. Dinners for Company at 12:00 noon.
First Section will move off at 1:30 p.m.

4. RATIONS.— Parties will be at THE FACTORY, CROISILLES, about 4:00 p.m. daily.
WATER.— Teams at R.I.1 and 2 and R.S.1 and 2. can obtain water from ECOUST.

                                        Falshaw Allnut   Captain.
                                          Commanding
                                          47th M.G. Coy.

Issued at 10:15 a.m.
Copy No. 1 and 2 . War Diary.
       3.   .   .   C.O.
       4.   .   .   2nd in Command.
       5.   .   .   O.C. A Section.
       6.   .   .   O.C. B Section.
       7.   .   .   O.C. C Section.
       8.   .   .   O.C. D Section.
       9.   .   .   D.M.G.O.
      10.   .   .   Retained.

Summary of Part taken by

No 41. M.G. Coy.

in Operations of the 16th inst.
_____

Ref. Map.
 Freizenberg 1/10,000.
_____

16. Guns of this Company were placed, in batterys of 4, at the following points.

D. 25. a. 25. 55.

D. 25. a. 5. 4.

D. 25 a. 25. 15.

D. 25 c 40. 65.

These opened fire at Zero on No 1 barrage line & continued firing till Zero +1.50 on the different barrage line laid down by

D.M.C.O. During the firing the enemy put down an Artillery Barrage on line occupied by Machine Guns this increased in intensity until zero + 1.50 when owing to casualties the Officer incharge of guns near crossroads Frezenburg decided to move forward.

This battery had orders to place 2 Guns at Vampir but Officer incharge received information that the enemy were still in possession of this place and consequently placed his guns in an old German Gun emplacement at D.25.a.0.4.

Here he dug in immediately behind

the emplacement which offered excellent cover & proceeded to bring up S.A.A. from Freigenberg.

According to O.O.O. 2 Guns from D.25.a.3.4. were to proceed to Bovy. Farm but as this place had not been captured these Guns were held in reserve and laid on their S.O.S. lines.

During the morning the S.O.S. was sent up and all guns opened intense rapid fire on S.O.S. barrage lines for 15 minutes thereafter reducing to a steady rate of fire for a further hour.

Parties of the enemy were seen advancing over the Tonnebeck Ridge and were engaged with apparent good results the observation being excellent.

Owing to the unexpected turn which the operations had taken all guns now only amounting to 10 were placed on the original 1st barrage lines instead of on the S.O.S. lines

Owing to the very large number of casualties which the Company had suffered it was found very difficult to man all the guns and at the same time maintain supply of bulk ammunition

About 9. pm. the 'S.O.S.' was again sent up and rapid fire was opened on No 1 barrage line.

The night of the 11th and the following day were more or less quiet.

At midnight on the 14th on instructions from the D.M.G.O. all positions occupied by us were evacuated and the Company withdrawn to the camp at Vlamertinghe.

Our total casualties during the 48 hours amounted to :-

      6 Killed
      1 Died of Wounds
      1 Missing
      24 Wounded.

also.   1 Killed
         11 Wounded

from carrying party of the
1st Royal Munster Fusiliers attached.

WAR DIARY.

FOR MONTH OF AUGUST, 1917.

VOLUME 18

UNIT 47B. Machine Gun Company
M.G. Corps

Army Form C. 2118.

WAR DIARY
or
INTELLIGENCE SUMMARY. 41st MACHINE GUN Coy
(Erase heading not required.)

Place	Date	Hour	Summary of Events and Information	Remarks and references to Appendices
TRENCHES	1-9-17		No indirect fire took place during this period. A little direct fire was carried out on enemys front line. No rear lanes to as kept actively. Enemy Artillery active in retaliation for Stokes M.G. fire. Generally still fire. Enemy throughout the period. Casualties 1 O.R. wounded.	
"	5-9-17		Coy carried on temporarily & rebuilding emplacements & Trenches & erecting the Machine Gun Posts also building dugouts for Teams.	
"	6-9-17	From 10·0 p.m. to 3·30 a.m. the following lifts were carried out: R.T. 4 TRIDENT ALLEY 100 rds R.T. 6 FAG ALLEY 100 rds Enemy M.G. Retaliation has been. Coy carried on as usual	

Army Form C. 2118.

WAR DIARY
or
INTELLIGENCE SUMMARY.
(Erase heading not required.)

Place	Date	Hour	Summary of Events and Information	Remarks and references to Appendices
TRENCHES	7-9-17		Slight increase in Enemy T.M. activity - Front line shelled in spots V14.a. No indirect M.G. activity. An enemy airplane shot flares over our lines dropped at 6.30 am. So very quiet. After a short interval the plane returned & it was driven at an increased speed. Continued patrols on U.G.'s & at emplacements day + night.	
"	8-9-17		Enemy again active with artillery & M.G. fire with increased front attack aimed at Kin high. M.G. tripod message in code gun crews in the support trenches are shared fire (one shot burst) & the patrols have cleaned all to our front again. Indirect fire carried out at V14.b.27. FAG ALLEY 1500 rounds. V14.b.25. V15.a.73 SUNKEN ROAD 750 rounds.	

WAR DIARY
or
INTELLIGENCE SUMMARY.

(Erase heading not required.)

Army Form C. 2118.

Place	Date	Hour	Summary of Events and Information	Remarks and references to Appendices
TRENCHES	8-9-17		Enemy retaliation very weak. We continued wiring as they were dispersed by our patrols at all points.	K
TRENCHES	9-9-17	8:00 a.m.	47th Brigade moved at same time as 63.	
		11:20 to 11:50 a.m.	Bombardment of enemy front line.	
			Will review gap projectiles on this front.	
			Artillery Co-operation at 2010 + 3 minutes barrage.	
			C.T.S. would fire for 13 mins a W.F. of gas.	
			Gas cloud all points.	
			Later we intend to burst up in FARNLEY and 200 rounds Gun shrapnel on trenches in U.S.L. enemy wire.	
			R. 100 rounds	
		7:00 p.m.	Our enemy commenced to shell RAILWAY RESERVE LINE 77 set guns shells	
		11:00 p.m.	10-00 p.m. enemy barrage from a half	

WAR DIARY
or
INTELLIGENCE SUMMARY.
(Erase heading not required.)

Army Form C. 2118.

Place	Date	Hour	Summary of Events and Information	Remarks and references to Appendices
TRENCHES	9/9/17		Our lines hill 70. TMs rifle grenades 77 + HEs very active on support & total enemy Ss. In addition a big amount of sector was sent over our lines. Enemy were very active towards Bruts was set to report. The enemy artillery replied vigorously, no hostility effective. Our own wiring at 11.10 p.m. Lab carried a big 28 Lewis guns over S.Ps	
TRENCHES	10.9.17		Enemy artillery chiefly increased somewhat during night to two towards our lines at 5.30 a.m. Enemy heavy day as for tourism. Guns attached at 7.30 p.m. Front line on the front. Enemy airplane continual working in all quarts etc.	Staff of List

WAR DIARY
or
INTELLIGENCE SUMMARY.

Army Form C. 2118.

(Erase heading not required.)

Place	Date	Hour	Summary of Events and Information	Remarks and references to Appendices
TRENCHES	11-9-17		Hostile Artillery quiet. Involved fire opened on Throughout the night. Artillery Engd:- Fdg ALLEY V.14.b 80.78 – 100 rds U.14.b 30.40 – 100 rds	
			1970 rounds fired at enemy emplmts. Hostile M.G.s active. 6 S.O.S. continuously observed	
TRENCHES	12-9-17		Hostile Artillery Shells Strong Support Systems Trench heavy afternoon with M.G. fire 9h25. Slight retaliation on T.M. S.O.S. carried out gas during the night. Enemy sniping at Railway Embankment working parties. Working on ell. craters & dugouts.	

WAR DIARY
or
INTELLIGENCE SUMMARY.

Army Form C. 2118.

Place	Date	Hour	Summary of Events and Information	Remarks and references to Appendices
TRENCHES	13.9.17		Hostile artillery shelled our support line during morning. Our artillery retaliated & in turn enemy shelled the F.A. & Red Marsh with H.E. &MG Search Fire. 10=0 hours Hostile 11=15 p.m. 9 R.I. team 600 rounds Lewis gun fire direct at U.S.C. @ 15° 9 1600 rounds DA 9 enemy bomb at 475.9023 Continued bombs Lewis lively afterwards. W.G. V.G.G.	
TRENCHES	14.9.17		Stokes artillery heavy shell fire shortly after midnight. 10=0 rounds from 676.80 2/(TRACK) Lancaster charge ??? been declared quiet. Hostiles fired RI 49 RI 5 gun fire 750 & 80 H.E. respectively FAG ALLEY (W.14.B) & Track in U.21.a & U.13.C. RI 5 also fired 500 rounds to the outskirts U.S.C. 00 15. M.G. fire covered at our ??? Portuguese.	

Army Form C. 2118.

WAR DIARY
or
INTELLIGENCE SUMMARY.
(Erase heading not required.)

Place	Date	Hour	Summary of Events and Information	Remarks and references to Appendices
TRENCHES	14.9.17		C.O.B. R.F.I. shot into the position both sides with bombs & enemy shells. Several H.E. & trench mortars.	
TRENCHES	15.9.17		Enemy artillery active during day. Enemy H.E. fire. Our trench mortars carried on at Yellow. R.T.6 – 100 rounds, C.B.C. 10.15, C.T. R.S.8 – 2500, U.7.6, 8.2, pm 15 pdr. Continued work on M.G. posts on day C.B. Four gun attacks by six M.G. left side raised enemy lights twice 4–10 p.m. & 8–00 p.m. Gun carried out harassing fire during night 14/15. Co-operated at the preliminary bombardment. The raid was a success, 21 prisoners, 1 M.G. & 1 automatic rifle were captured. Guns also co-operated in bombardment will bar barrage at 4.50 a.m. Jeb & Alfred Hurst	

WAR DIARY
or
INTELLIGENCE SUMMARY.
(Erase heading not required.)

Army Form C. 2118.

Place	Date	Hour	Summary of Events and Information	Remarks and references to Appendices
TRENCHES	15.9.17		Held on the same front. Enemy shelling of the 16th Casualties nil	
TRENCHES	16.9.17		Found hostile artillery v.l. of fire R.1 5 fired 100 rounds on enemy tracks & O.Ts during night. Enemy aeroplane dropped 4 bombs at 7.30 p.m. about 100 yds in rear of our 6.6 O.P. caused no damage.	
TRENCHES	17.9.17		Battery received replies from their guns R.1 6 & R.1 6. Co-operated in S.O.S F.M. Bombardment by Enemy Canada at 2.30 p.m. 4.00 a.m. shrapnel fired enemy trench system, direction beyond enemy front line. R.S.3 fired 2,500 rds. Enemy night S.O.S S.O.S at U.7.6.8.2. Carried out 6.6b at intervals	

J. Bassett Lieut

WAR DIARY
or
INTELLIGENCE SUMMARY.
(Erase heading not required.)

Army Form C. 2118.

Place	Date	Hour	Summary of Events and Information	Remarks and references to Appendices
TRENCHES	18.9.17		Hostile Artillery v.G. of fire. Shelled several of our U.S. positions. 1 E.A. attacked the Inf AMB 255 rds Infantry to Sections. No casualties at all positions.	
TRENCHES	19.9.17		Enemy Activity firing a Gas Cloud at night. Wireless activity normal. Guns fired as follows— R.T. 344 650 78 gr SOS lines R.T. 346 6250 " Enemy C.T. & Lights R.T. 2 570 " at Enemy aeroplane shot noted our lines at 5:40 p.m. L.O.B. continued U.G. Nos Events Aug 18.	
TRENCHES	20.9.17		Enemy Artillery fairly quiet. Aircraft Active & flares noted over lines during day. 1 E.A. wounded Artillery Observer over A.M.G.	Appendix hereto

Army Form C. 2118.

WAR DIARY
or
INTELLIGENCE SUMMARY.
(Erase heading not required.)

Instructions regarding War Diaries and Intelligence Summaries are contained in F. S. Regs., Part II. and the Staff Manual respectively. Title pages will be prepared in manuscript.

Place	Date	Hour	Summary of Events and Information	Remarks and references to Appendices
TRENCHES	20.9.17		Enemy Quiet night R7.5 & R7.6 shed Bom Cd a FAP ALLEY & Enemy trench in U.B.C. Still working on N.G. Nob & Rounds	
TRENCHES	21.9.17		Enemy Activity active throughout period Hostile M.G. worked Oct M.G.s R.y.5.96. find 3x0 no to U.19.C.22.20. Our MG's let us know near of enemy line. Enemy aircraft active with bombs in large no Ms. to 3 occasions. Our own working in large no's there of	
TRENCHES	22.9.17		Hostile Artillery shewed increased activity day & night. His Aircraft very active. Brought day activity very good & any calm. R7.5.& 6 flare Boro Round by Enemy trench	

[signature]

WAR DIARY
or
INTELLIGENCE SUMMARY.
(Erase heading not required.)

Army Form C. 2118.

Place	Date	Hour	Summary of Events and Information	Remarks and references to Appendices
TRENCHES	23.9.14		Heavy Artillery very quiet throughout the day. Sniped at in various parts of our trenches. Slight HER. as being experienced. Work of trenches & entanglements & HER carried on as per S.O.W.O.	
TRENCHES	24.9.14		Heavy Artillery of Nature firing for activity. Notably in our trenches. No activity from MG aircraft. Firing on followed by the bats. W.O. Inflated 15th Rus. S. Communication trench 14.35 Rus. Aircraft active every evening. 1 E.A. driven off by A.A. M.G. fire.	
TRENCHES	25.9.14		Enemy Artillery activity confined to desultory shelling at intervals during day & night.	

A6045 Wt. W11422/M1160 350,000 12/16 D. D. & L. Forms/C./2118/14

WAR DIARY
or
INTELLIGENCE SUMMARY.
(Erase heading not required.)

Army Form C. 2118.

Place	Date	Hour	Summary of Events and Information	Remarks and references to Appendices
TRENCHES	25-9-17		Contd. 4000 rds were fired during night by R.T. 5-96. Sent to enemy. 2150 those shells & by front line system. Relieve almost nil. Was continued as before.	
TRENCHES	26.9.17		Hostile Artillery active against back areas chiefly. Coy H.Q. at T.30.a.11. Shelled in afternoon till H.E. a little away being done to iron work & link hut in forest. Great deal of yellow R.T. of 2000 rds. FAG ALLEY R.T. 6,200. U.S. central searchlight Section club crowd got in afternoon. Casualties 1 O.R. wounded.	
TRENCHES	27.9.17		Usual intermittent shelling by Enemy. Our M.G. Co-operated in Bombardment by Artillery & H.T.M.S at 3.10 p.m. 17,000 rds being fired with burst	

WAR DIARY
or
INTELLIGENCE SUMMARY.
(Erase heading not required.)

Army Form C. 2118.

Place	Date	Hour	Summary of Events and Information	Remarks and references to Appendices
TRENCHES	27.9.17		Cont... find various selected targets in rear of Enemy front line system. Work continued on L.G. post in under dugouts.	
TRENCHES	28.9.17		Hostile Artillery comparatively quiet. Enemy was observed working in and moving about the various M.G. positions at times during night, but declined to retaliate at times. 3 E.A. crossed our lines at 5.30 p.m. Very heavy fire at by the A.A.M.G. 500 rounds being expended. General Stand to but Rodger A company reinforced front line to hold at night. Artillery developed intensive fire on and at night. Artillery developed Guns fired on CRUMP ALLEY during night & roads leading to BULOW & RODER. Accounts of heavy expended to work on account of General "Stand To".	

J. Shapurji Lieut

WAR DIARY
or
INTELLIGENCE SUMMARY
(Erase heading not required.)

Army Form C. 2118.

Place	Date	Hour	Summary of Events and Information	Remarks and references to Appendices
TRENCHES	29.9.17		Hostile Artillery quiet. 11 O.R's. per 2/5th Hampshire Regt. Light but sustained hostile machine gun fire. Disposn. was as follows:- 3/9ᵗʰ 8500 Cubits. Enemy Crenulation Trenches 3/9ᵗʰ during night 393 Turned Gun. Ammunition Us (?) Enemy Post Line System (F.A.G. ALLEY) trench U.21.b. 95.55 & U.15.c. 90.60 during night 2000 rounds fired. Our enemy snipers active during day. Wire at 6.0 p.m. the above allotted to our A.A.M.G. took the W.G.R-A-Ampos continued.	
TRENCHES	30.9.17		Enemy Artillery & M.G. fire normal. but aircraft active both day & night. 3 Scouts seen dropped U.19. at 6.45 p.m. but no damage ... Despond Post Corner trench 394 × 392 fired 4.750 rounds. M. U.21.b. 20.80. Enemy active ...	

Army Form C. 2118.

WAR DIARY
or
INTELLIGENCE SUMMARY.
(Erase heading not required.)

Instructions regarding War Diaries and Intelligence Summaries are contained in F. S. Regs., Part II. and the Staff Manual respectively. Title pages will be prepared in manuscript.

Place	Date	Hour	Summary of Events and Information	Remarks and references to Appendices
RENNES	30.9.17		[illegible handwritten entry]	

WAR   DIARY

FOR MONTH OF OCTOBER, 1917.

UNIT 47th Machine Gun Coy.

VOLUME NUMBER 19

No 47 Machine Gun Coy.

War Diary
for
October, 1917.

```
47TH M. G. COY.
No. W.D. X.'17
Date 31: 10: 17
```

WAR DIARY
or
INTELLIGENCE SUMMARY.

Army Form C. 2118.

Place	Date	Hour	Summary of Events and Information	Remarks and references to Appendices
TRENCHES	1-8-17		Hostile Artillery quiet. 5 unexploded trench mortars. Trident Sa crashed nr. Yellow Sqa 1, Sqa 2, 6, no cas.s. nr. TRIDENT ALLEY, & FAG ALLEY. O.R.s caused no cas. on previous G.	
TRENCHES	2-8-17		Hostile Artillery & Machine Gun fire normal. Our Artillery carried out an organised shoot on Trident Sell Strain U.14.a. U & lo & Co's front. Heavy S.O.S. went up Artillery Target FAG ALLEY fired on during night & no rounds expended. O.R.s continued. R.U.S. Work. G.	
TRENCHES	3-8-17		Hostile Artillery quiet. No enemy trench mortars on account of baths. Heavy Sound Enemy Sell. Strom amount of S.A.A. carried up to W.S. line. O.R.s continued with trenches, dugouts, & emplacements.	

J. Stapres Lieut

Army Form C. 2118.

WAR DIARY
or
INTELLIGENCE SUMMARY.
(Erase heading not required.)

Place	Date	Hour	Summary of Events and Information	Remarks and references to Appendices
TRENCHES	4-10-17		Enemy continued quiet, all Co's first as yesterday. Enemy Shell Bty in (U.14.a.) to do some damage. Continued working on dug out. Lieut. a. Chuff got up. Rest to GEENSLANE	
TRENCHES	5-10-17		Enemy activity normal. All Co's fired during night to U.8.C. 95.97. 6,000 rounds being fired. Work continued of MG positions.	
TRENCHES	6-10-17		An argument shot was opened out by the artillery. C. S. with the object of deceiving the enemy, simulating an attack, and ascertain how he put down a defensive barrage. Also to ascertain what grounds he had covering his Batn + So for the Coys M.G's for Signals working to Barrage 95.00 Raids by assault Infr. working in conjunction the afternoon action between by	J. Shaffield Sweet

Army Form C. 2118.

WAR DIARY
or
INTELLIGENCE SUMMARY.
(Erase heading not required.)

Instructions regarding War Diaries and Intelligence Summaries are contained in F. S. Regs., Part II. and the Staff Manual respectively. Title pages will be prepared in manuscript.

Place	Date	Hour	Summary of Events and Information	Remarks and references to Appendices
TRENCHES	6-10-17		Enemy trench mortars and MG shots. Retaliating by our arty. 6700 rds of S.A.A. fired by M.G. Coy to rob enemy working.	
TRENCHES	7-10-17		Enemy quiet. April 8 front line in inclement at dawn. Our arty active with our S.A.A at all periodical intervals during night.	
TRENCHES	8-10-17		Enemy again quiet. 800 Aus8 New York R, F.A. Regt Inf. Cd respond from 12.45 to 1.15 p.m. by MG.B&D at C.20.62.17. SUNKEN ROAD U.2.a – U.8.a. Our artillery bombardment 10.00 enemy heavy strict Retaliation crossroads. Rob enemy W at work.	
TRENCHES	9-A-17		Little activity shewn. The Bn^r is relieved by Reserve Regt. relief complete by eight Army Coy to rob plus Rob carried out uneventfully. Respectively.	

Army Form C. 2118.

WAR DIARY
or
INTELLIGENCE SUMMARY.
(Erase heading not required.)

Instructions regarding War Diaries and Intelligence Summaries are contained in F. S. Regs., Part II, and the Staff Manual respectively. Title pages will be prepared in manuscript.

Place	Date	Hour	Summary of Events and Information	Remarks and references to Appendices
TRENCHES	11.10.17		Enemy artillery quiet. Bombs used in FRA & TRIDENT ALLEY. Enemy M.Gs active throughout the night. Enemy's wire & ours cut.	
TRENCHES	12.10.17		Hostile Artillery very active during evening. Our front line subjected to barrage. Enemy M.G. during the night. Enemy attempted to raid a post during the night, but beaten off. Enemy in enemy trench – prisoner with Rifle Grenades – one enemy wounded. Our casualties – one slightly wounded. 28.08 rounds fired.	
TRENCHES	13.10.17		Activity on part of Enemy increased. Our information agents & prisoners' evidence that the Enemy intend some retaliation for our front line break-through. L.A. Coys at work at night.	

WAR DIARY
or
INTELLIGENCE SUMMARY

Army Form C. 2118.

(Erase heading not required.)

Instructions regarding War Diaries and Intelligence Summaries are contained in F.S. Regs., Part II. and the Staff Manual respectively. Title pages will be prepared in manuscript.

Place	Date	Hour	Summary of Events and Information	Remarks and references to Appendices
TRENCHES	14/11/17		Enemy Artillery & M.G. action. Guns quiet. Our quiet. Enemy Artillery sent a few rounds into FORTIFIED SHELL HOLES (C.14.A) 6pm. Continued.	
TRENCHES	15/11/17		Hostile Artillery & M.G. quiet. Our Artillery active. Enemy sent a few Artillery M.G. & specials into the C.T.s & junction 8000 road find. M.G. post at Co Central Keep area.	
TRENCHES	16/11/17		Hostile Activity continued normal. A lieutenant & Artillery & M.G. and Enemy sent at 4.00 p.m. one fork in Epruich High at yellow cross Trench. SUNKEN ROAD in C.8.a.? Enemy being found. Retaliation was sent & suspected Artillery copy in Shaft Dugouts, emplacements & M.G. RAL.	

[signed] J. R. Mulholland Lieut

WAR DIARY or INTELLIGENCE SUMMARY

Army Form C. 2118.

(Erase heading not required.)

Place	Date	Hour	Summary of Events and Information	Remarks and references to Appendices
TRENCHES	17-10-17		Hostile Artillery active during last night firing Barrage "A.A." over head ceasing at 10:00 a.m. Our Artillery Offrs. in observations + M.G. fire + 4000 rounds I.C.A.H. every up to time	
TRENCHES	18-10-17		Artillery of all Cos. quiet. T.M. active at night. Gas shells fired on CROSS ROADS at U.15.d. 85, 95. during night. Work as usual	
TRENCHES	19-10-17		Usual Artillery fire. World from line. Our M.G.s fired on S.15.c. 86, 86. — 470 rounds Work continued. Slight air-aeroplanes observed.	
TRENCHES	20-10-17		Enemy Artillery active. Aircraft cruised over lines at 4:30 am & 1:50 rounds fired by our A.A.M.G. Enemy fired on battery at U.14 & 6.1 N.V.15. a.g.g. fired by	

Army Form C. 2118.

WAR DIARY
or
INTELLIGENCE SUMMARY.
(Erase heading not required.)

Instructions regarding War Diaries and Intelligence Summaries are contained in F. S. Regs., Part II. and the Staff Manual respectively. Title pages will be prepared in manuscript.

Place	Date	Hour	Summary of Events and Information	Remarks and references to Appendices
TRENCHES	21-10-17		Enemy artillery & M.G. fire active between 7 and 9 p.m. 1 = A food on at 10.45 a.m. No night firing as own patrols were out.	Ama.
"	22-10-17		Company relieved by 48th M.G. Coy. as per attached operation order.	Ama.
ERVILLERS	23-10-17		Company in Camp. Overhauling & cleaning all guns and gun equipment.	Ama.
	24-10-17 } 28-10-17 }		Do. Improving camp generally and working on instruments, starts —	Ama.
	29-10-17		Do. Preparing guns and gun equipment for trenches. Cleaning and refilling at belts. Repacking fighting limbers.	Ama.
	30-10-17		Company relieved 49th M.G. Coy in left sector of Divisional front. 16 guns taken over. Relief reported complete 1-30 p.m. No night firing.	Ama.
	31-10-17		Line quiet. Barrage fire in support of artillery bombardment. 2800 rounds fired	Ama.

Joseph Andrew
Capt
OC 47th MG Coy

Copy No 9.

No 47 Machine Gun Company.

Operation Order No 105.

Coy. HQ.   21-10-17.

1. No 47 M.G. Coy will be relieved tomorrow, 22nd inst, by No 48 M.G. Coy.

2. One Guide from Left Group will be at the FACTORY, CROISELLES at 2:30 p.m. to guide limbers of 48th M.G. Coy to Left Section HQ.
   One Guide per Team with the exception of those at 70 central and TIGER TRENCH will be at Left Section HQ. at 3:00 p.m.

3. Transport to convey Guns &c, will be at 39th position at 3:30 p.m. where Teams will load up, thereafter proceeding by sections to camp at ERVILLERS.

4. Guns at 70 central and TIGER TRENCH will relieve independently as soon as dark.

5. The following will be handed over and receipts in duplicate, signed by both parties obtained:—

   Tripods.   Over Boards.
   Belt Boxes.   Range Cards.
   S.O.S. buckets.   Aiming Discs.
   Foolproofs.   Water Cans.
   Work on hand.   Work to be done.

                                J. Sheffield, Lt/Captain.
                                    Commanding
                                    47th M.G. Coy.

Copy No
1. C.O.
2. 2nd in Command.
3. O.C. Left Group.
4. O.C. Centre Group.
5. O.C. Right Group.
6. Lieut. Whitehead.
7. Lieut. Burns. (T.O.)
8. 48th M.G. Coy.
9 and 10. War Diary.

WAR DIARY

FOR MONTH OF NOVEMBER, 1917.

VOLUME :- 20
UNIT :- 4th Machine Gun Company

No. 47 Machine Gun Coy.

War Diary.

November. 1917.

WAR DIARY or INTELLIGENCE SUMMARY

Army Form C. 2118.

Place	Date	Hour	Summary of Events and Information	Remarks and references to Appendices
TRENCHES	1-11-17		Hostile Artillery slightly intermittently throughout day. Enemy M.G. fire during night, but not in such volume. Our line 30 Div. to Cerise Target detect enemy fire system during night. 6th Infantry Bde went into Corps Reserve billets, right flank Jordan. Relieved commenced 6.45 A.	
TRENCHES	2-11-17		Enemy Artillery continued active during night. Le Brigade Gel at 9.0 p.m. Artillery, M.G. Greenapolet shoot. Limit D. final U.2.d. 7.9 9.0 p.m. 1650 U.2.a. 4.5.7.8 1650 U.2.c. 2o.13 1350 Enemy party (Estimated 40 O.R.) approach Redan Ordered. Trench trammeled & captured to us. Successful.	J. Stafford Lieut.

WAR DIARY or INTELLIGENCE SUMMARY

Army Form C. 2118.

Place	Date	Hour	Summary of Events and Information	Remarks and references to Appendices
TRENCHES	6-11-17		Both Artilleries active. M.G. active. L.G. Opened a bombardment will. Our artillery at 12.0 a.m. & our again at 12.20 a.m. on Chyrens hill. Artillery and M.G. fire in retaliation was immediate. Artillery fire on G. Co. front B.T.B. sent forward at 12.3 a.m. Our guns co-operated in Bn. Artillery Barrage & on enemy's front lines.	
TRENCHES	7-11-17		Both Artilleries active. M.G. quieter than usual. Our guns carried out more night firing. 200 rounds expended on C.T. and tracks in rear of enemy's lines into our front M.G. barrage position.	
TRENCHES	8-11-17		Both Artillery comparatively quiet all & active to left. Shower during the day. Our guns maintained their activity during night in order to co-operate in hindrance wise strong-points fixed task continued. J. Shadfield Lieut

WAR DIARY
or
INTELLIGENCE SUMMARY.

Army Form C. 2118.

(Erase heading not required.)

Place	Date	Hour	Summary of Events and Information	Remarks and references to Appendices
TRENCHES	9-11-17		Enemy artillery slightly active during day. This evening artillery of our Grenadiers H.Q. & co-operated with increase in the artillery fire to harass enemy during night. A Co. found 2000 rounds of S.A.A. carried up to the line. B Co. relieved.	
TRENCHES	10-11-17		Hostile artillery inactive. M.G. increased activity during night. Men are viewing and found relief in C.T.'s & troops thought right L.S.R. in support. D relieved.	
TRENCHES	11-11-17		Hostile artillery active throughout day. Enemy a successful gas & smoke barrage launched by Canad. inf at 7.30am against TUNNEL TRENCH. A good show was formed which hung over the enemy line for a considerable time. Hostile retaliation was slight. Our guns co-operated & a slow harassing fire [?] was kept up [?]	

WAR DIARY
or
INTELLIGENCE SUMMARY

Army Form C. 2118.

Place	Date	Hour	Summary of Events and Information	Remarks and references to Appendices
TRENCHES	12-11-17		Hostile Artillery active M.G. & sniper Vickers gun fired 2,500 rounds in C.T. & blocky behind enemy line during night. Took up barrage positions, battalion still out. Trenches continued. 60,000 rounds of S.A.A. taken up to barrage positions.	
TRENCHES	13-11-17		Artillery & M.G. comparatively quiet. No night firing by hun. Took up barrage positions & carried 40,000 rounds of S.A.A. to same.	
TRENCHES	14-11-17		Company relieved by 49 M.G. Coy. On completion of relief Coy proceeded to camp at ERVILLERS. Noted remainder of day.	
ERVILLERS	15-11-17		Parade as follows — Cleaning guns & gun equipment	
ERVILLERS	17-11-17		Overhauling S.A.A. and web load belts. Church parade. Nominal list	

WAR DIARY
or
INTELLIGENCE SUMMARY

Army Form C. 2118.

Place	Date	Hour	Summary of Events and Information	Remarks and references to Appendices
TRENCHES	18.11.17.			
TRENCHES	20.11.17		About 16 M.G. took part during operations 20/21 Nov. 9=0 p.m. Company march into line and occupied Barrage positions 4 guns placed at V.25.a.4. and 12 guns along RAILWAY EMBANKMENT (V.26.c.5.3.4.3.7.) 6.20.a.m. Fire was opened and sustained until 7.50am Barrels were then changed. Guns cleaned and elevations. 7.20.am. Four Guns opened fire on Special targets at V.15.c.d.d. 8.35.am. Guns switched back on to Barrage line in response to S.O.S. Signal given left of Division's Front. Positions fire was maintained for 35 minutes. Thereafter gradually reducing until 9.30 am. When fire ceased. The 4 Guns were then put back on to Special targets. J. Stanfield Lieut	

Army Form C. 2118.

WAR DIARY
or
INTELLIGENCE SUMMARY.
(Erase heading not required.)

Place	Date	Hour	Summary of Events and Information	Remarks and references to Appendices
TRENCHES	20-11-17		Cold.	
		12-n noon	Huns were firing MG's back R.F. and fired on telephone wires	
			in VULCAN TRENCH the Corps & Brigadier General	
		3-35 p.m.	Barrage again (reported to S.O.S. Line on enemy	
			Artillery becoming very active	
		4-10 p.m.	Ceased fire.	
		4-40 p.m.	No 5 Group switched on to SUNKEN ROAD	
			in U.14.6. The night 20/21 was quiet	
TRENCHES	21-11-17	6-30 a.m.	Guns not now opened R. Barrage line in	
			Copse to S.O.S. and ceased fire at	
		7:30 a.m.	when situation became normal	
		1-45 p.m.	orders received from Div. G.O. to occupy	
			(Regton) Emplacements in River f Scarfold	
				Lieut.

Army Form C. 2118.

WAR DIARY
or
INTELLIGENCE SUMMARY.
(Erase heading not required.)

Instructions regarding War Diaries and Intelligence Summaries are contained in F. S. Regs., Part II. and the Staff Manual respectively. Title pages will be prepared in manuscript.

Place	Date	Hour	Summary of Events and Information	Remarks and references to Appendices
TRENCHES	21-11-17	Cult.		
		6:10 pm	Stores complete, and guns laid in their Barrage Line. Ammunition expenditure 20/21 Nov 220,000 rounds. Casualties - Nil.	
TRENCHES	22-11-17	4=0 am.	S.O.S. showed on left. Guns opened out and maintained intense fire until situation appeared normal. 8000 rounds fired this night from No 3 place in accent of our patrols leaving any action.	
TRENCHES	23-11-17		Enemy comparatively quiet. Our M.G. Coy greater all withdrawn in support. A party of Infantry took attacked. Captured & consolidated the MEBU NOSE and TUNNEL from U.20 & 32.90 to U.20 & 52.76. 1 M.G., 1 Wurmberger & 21 prisoners were captured.	

Army Form C. 2118.

WAR DIARY
or
INTELLIGENCE SUMMARY.
(Erase heading not required.)

Instructions regarding War Diaries and Intelligence Summaries are contained in F. S. Regs., Part II. and the Staff Manual respectively. Title pages will be prepared in manuscript.

Place	Date	Hour	Summary of Events and Information	Remarks and references to Appendices
TRENCHES	24-11-17		Hostile Artillery quiet during day. At 8.80 p.m. he did a little trench mortar activity. Whole guns were cleared up. Barrage position. S.A.A. carried up.	
TRENCHES	25-11-17		Hostile Artillery much quieter. Artillery much reported from line. No night firing took place. Working in explosives today at S.	
TRENCHES	26-11-17		Hostile Artillery comparatively quiet. Our M.G. fired 12,500 rounds during night - Burns tracks of C.T.s behind enemy line on account of suspected Enemy Relief.	
TRENCHES	27-11-17		Slight activity on part of Enemy. Our guns did not fire as Strong patrols were out. Winogradow tried to explore enemy trenches, & dugouts, [illegible] [illegible]	

D. D. & L., London, E.C.
(A800) Wt W1771/M2931 750,000 5/17 Sch. 33 Forms/C2118/14

Army Form C. 2118.

WAR DIARY
or
INTELLIGENCE SUMMARY.
(Erase heading not required.)

Place	Date	Hour	Summary of Events and Information	Remarks and references to Appendices
TRENCHES	28-11-17		Enemy activity on the increase. Our guns have been active during period. S.A.A. served up to all positions. Both continued at all positions.	
TRENCHES	29-11-17	5=35 a.m. 7=0 a.m. 7.00	S.O.S. observed. Relief finished. Silence opened around. Relief finished. Remainder temporary quiet. Work on Trenches, dug-outs, emplacements Continued.	
TRENCHES	30-11-17		Enemy Artillery very active throughout day. Direct hit were obtained by him on two emplacements. Our own Army bombardment in early morning.	E Skattney Lieut

Army Form C. 2118.

WAR DIARY
or
INTELLIGENCE SUMMARY.
(Erase heading not required.)

Place	Date	Hour	Summary of Events and Information	Remarks and references to Appendices
TRENCHES	30-11-17		Quiet. Our guns 5.00 am & at 6.00 am & S.O.S. line. Hos Infantry action followed. Work continued to emplacements, trenches & dug outs. J. Sponford Lieut.	

WAR DIARY,

FOR MONTH OF DECEMBER, 1917.

VOLUME :- 21

UNIT :- 4/5 Machine Gun Company.

No. 47 Machine Gun Coy.

War Diary.

DECEMBER. 1917.

Army Form C. 2118.

WAR DIARY
or
INTELLIGENCE SUMMARY.
(Erase heading not required.)

Instructions regarding War Diaries and Intelligence Summaries are contained in F. S. Regs., Part II. and the Staff Manual respectively. Title pages will be prepared in manuscript.

Place	Date	Hour	Summary of Events and Information	Remarks and references to Appendices
TRENCHES	1-12-17		Hostile Artillery active throughout period. 5-30 a.m. Enemy heavily bombarded front system 1, with all calibre. Machine Guns opened fire & S.O.S. lines in short bursts. 7.00 a.m. defensive guns closed for R Quarter. Becoming normal.	
TRENCHES	2-12-17		Enemy continued active with Artillery, Machine Gun. Enemy particularly active about 4=00 a.m. Guns swept sprinkled our S.O.S. Lines 18,000 round fired. No hostile Infantry action followed. Guns ceased fire later. Situation appeared normal. Company relieved at night by 119 U.S. Inf. & Coy R Company relief by us opposed & Coys at GOMIECOURT S.D.	
GOMIECOURT	3-12-17		Company cleaned S.D. 1=30 p.m. Company paraded in Full Marching Order Sheffield Kent	

D. D. & L. London, E.C.
(A8049) Wt W1771/M2053 750,000 5/17 Sch. 53 Forms/C/2118/14

Army Form C. 2118.

WAR DIARY
or
INTELLIGENCE SUMMARY.
(Erase heading not required.)

Instructions regarding War Diaries and Intelligence Summaries are contained in F. S. Regs., Part II. and the Staff Manual respectively. Title pages will be prepared in manuscript.

Place	Date	Hour	Summary of Events and Information	Remarks and references to Appendices
GOMIECOURT	3-12-17		1-45 p.m. Coy moved off and marched to BEAULENCOURT via SAPIGNIES – BAPAUME	
			5-30 p.m. Coy arrived at Billets in BEAULENCOURT and H.Q. Established at the Coy (later Bn) winter quarter of Roy.	
BEAULENCOURT	4-12-17		Company had a general clean up of guns & gun equipment, S.D.	
BEAULENCOURT	5-12-17		Lewis Gun inspected, and all transport looked, cleaned and oiled.	
BEAULENCOURT	6-12-17		9-0 a.m. Coy paraded in Full Marching Order, and marched to TINCOURT via ROCQUIGNY – MANANCOURT MOISLANS – TEMPLEUX-la-FOSSE Company arrived	

D. D. & L. London, E.C.
(A5049) W1 W1777/M2091 750,000 5/17 Sch. 33 Forms/C2118/11

Army Form C. 2118.

WAR DIARY
or
INTELLIGENCE SUMMARY.
(Erase heading not required.)

Place	Date	Hour	Summary of Events and Information	Remarks and references to Appendices
TINCOURT	6-12-17		Contd. in Billets at TINCOURT at 5.30 p.m. and H.Q. established at 1 DOVER ST	
TINCOURT	7-12-17		Company cleaned guns, gun equipment, & fighting Limbers packed ready for action. Company routed remainder of day.	
TINCOURT	8-12-17		Miscellaneous parades during day. 2-0 p.m. C & D Sections paraded to 8TH E MR IE & latter still in reserve	
TINCOURT	9-12-17	8.0 a.m.	A & B Sections proceed to line, & took up position in L'EMPIRE. C Section took up position in TETARD WOOD, & RAILWAY EMBANKMENT in F.1.a.8.1. D Section took up position in QUEUCHETTES WOOD.	Schofield Lieut

Army Form C. 2118.

WAR DIARY
or
INTELLIGENCE SUMMARY.
(Erase heading not required.)

Place	Date	Hour	Summary of Events and Information	Remarks and references to Appendices
TRENCHES	9-12-17		All guns were laid on S.O.C. lines ready to meet an attack	
TRENCHES	10-12-17		Hostile Artillery & M. Guns Guns active Shelling etc. in placements, shelter etc. Casualties 1 O.R. wounded	
TRENCHES	11-12-17		Artillery & Machine Guns activ on both sides. Looking to emplacements, trenches & shelter. 40 rds rounds R.S.A.A. expended up to present	
TRENCHES	12-12-17		Hostile Artillery active throughout point. Our Guns opened up a gas and fire on S.O.S. lines expending 5,000 rounds S.A.A. expended. Our Machine Guns were	
TRENCHES	13-12-17		Hostile Artillery active. Our Machine Guns were active on tracks & road leading to enemy lines. 300 rounds fired. 20,000 rds of S.A.A. expended up to present (twenty five)	

WAR DIARY
or
INTELLIGENCE SUMMARY.

Army Form C. 2118.

Place	Date	Hour	Summary of Events and Information	Remarks and references to Appendices
TRENCHES	14-12-17		Hostile activity has slight during [day?]. Our artillery K.R.R. [?] active but at all [positions?] [?]. Casualties 1 O.R. wounded	
TRENCHES	15-12-17		Company relieved by #8 M.G. Coy & #9 M.G. Coy. #8 M.G.Coy relieved platoon in QUEUCHETTES WOOD. #9 M.G.Coy relieved platoon in TETARD WOOD & RAILWAY EMBANKMENT. The L'EMPIRE here evacuated. R. Coy relieved & [?] to TINCOURT. Casualties 2 O.R. wounded.	
TINCOURT	16-12-17		Parade 9.0 a.m. — 12.30 p.m. Cleaning Guns & Gun equipment. Baths.	Schofield Lieut

Army Form C. 2118.

WAR DIARY
or
INTELLIGENCE SUMMARY.
(Erase heading not required.)

Instructions regarding War Diaries and Intelligence Summaries are contained in F. S. Regs., Part II. and the Staff Manual respectively. Title pages will be prepared in manuscript.

Place	Date	Hour	Summary of Events and Information	Remarks and references to Appendices
TINCOURT	17=12=17		Parade. 9.0 a.m. Company Inspection. 9.30 to 12.30. Gun Drill & Grenade Actn. 2.30 & 3=0 p.m. Gas Drill & Capt. G.F. Hall Inf. Res. our Command.	
TINCOURT	18=12=17		Parade. 9.0 a.m. Company Inspection. 9.30 to 12.30. Cleaning Guns & Gun equipment. All fighting kits in order. & Apparel.	
TINCOURT	19=12=17		Parade. 9.0 a.m. Company Inspection 9.30 to 12.30. Gun Drill & Grenade Actn. 2.30 to 3=0 p.m. Gas Drill.	

J. Shacklok Kent

WAR DIARY
or
INTELLIGENCE SUMMARY

Army Form C. 2118.

Place	Date	Hour	Summary of Events and Information	Remarks and references to Appendices
TINCOURT	20-12-17		Parade.	
		9.30 a.m.	Inspection by C.O. 10=0 a.m. to 12=0 noon. A & B. Coins Border practice. 2=0 pm & 4=0 pm C & D Section Border practice.	
			All Officers reconnoitred the line.	
TINCOURT	21-12-17		Company attended the 49 M.G. Coy as the line (Operation Order No 107) Relief complete by 5-30 p.m.	
TRENCHES	22-12-17		Hostile artillery active. A few Gas Shells fell near Cross Roads MALASSISE at 6.30 p.m. Our Guns fired 2.00 rounds at Target a.7.6.85.95 from 9=0 p.m. to 6=0 a.m. Work carried out at all positions.	

[signature]
Lieut

Army Form C. 2118.

WAR DIARY
or
INTELLIGENCE SUMMARY.
(Erase heading not required.)

Place	Date	Hour	Summary of Events and Information	Remarks and references to Appendices
TRENCHES	23-12-17		Hostile Artillery active throughout the night. Gun at 20.25 Breslin. Fire at J. notes. No reply also Our guns fired 300 rounds at targets a.7.b.75.60, a.7.b.75.30, and a.7.b.40.95, a.7.b.65.90. Continued work on emplacements, dug outs & tracks.	
TRENCHES	24-12-17		Hostile Artillery & aeroplanes very active. Hostile Guns fired at 6.0 rounds 1.50 p at a.7.b.40.95, a.7.b.65.90, n at a.7.b.95.55 to a.7.b.75.55 } during night 1.50 1000 rounds at & many targets	
TRENCHES	25-12-17		Hostile Artillery active throughout front. Heavy shelling during night. Our recent retaliated activity fire at La Bassée at 5.50 p.m. for 15 minutes Hostile fire opened at during night on the Yellow Line	

Army Form C. 2118.

WAR DIARY
or
INTELLIGENCE SUMMARY.
(Erase heading not required.)

Instructions regarding War Diaries and Intelligence Summaries are contained in F. S. Regs., Part II. and the Staff Manual respectively. Title pages will be prepared in manuscript.

Place	Date	Hour	Summary of Events and Information	Remarks and references to Appendices
TRENCHES	25-12-17		a.7b.75.80.9&7b.75.30. 1500 rounds a.14.a.10.14. 20.0 rounds. Work continued at all points.	
TRENCHES	26-12-17		Hostile Artillery & Machine Guns normal. Vickers Gun fired as follows:- 1500 rounds M a.14.a.10.12. 1500 " " a.14.05.24. 2.00 " " at Enemy Aircraft. Work carried out at all positions.	
TRENCHES	27-12-17		Hostile Artillery quiet during day. Slow steady shelling during night. Enemy Machine guns active. Vickers Guns fired as follows:- 1500 rounds M a.7b.40.95.6. a.7b.65.30. 1500 " " a.7b.65.50 & a.7b.75.30. Work continued.	

J. Stanfield
Lieut.

Army Form C. 2118.

WAR DIARY
or
INTELLIGENCE SUMMARY.
(Erase heading not required.)

Instructions regarding War Diaries and Intelligence Summaries are contained in F. S. Regs., Part II. and the Staff Manual respectively. Title pages will be prepared in manuscript.

Place	Date	Hour	Summary of Events and Information	Remarks and references to Appendices
TRENCHES	28-12-17		Enemy Caterpoeatively Quiet. Vickers Guns fired as follows:—	
			2,700 rounds in x 29 c. 17.35. & x 29 c. 12.31.	
			2,700 " " a 8 c. 10.10. " a 8 c. 10. 63. } during night	
			1,700 " " at Enemy Aircraft during day	
			Work continued at all positions	
TRENCHES	29-12-17		Hostile Artillery normal. Aircraft active during morning	
			Indirect fire covered at as follows:—	
			2,700 rounds in a. 7. 6.24. 90 & a. 1. d. 66. 13. } during night	
			2,700 " " a.14.c. 32.52. " a. 14.c. 22. 04 }	
			2,50 " " at Enemy Aircraft	
			Emplacement improved. 20.00 rounds S.A.A. expended	
			to Line	
				J Sheffield
				Lieut.

D. D. & L., London, E.C.
(A5041) Wt W4771/M2931 750,000 5/17 Sch. 52 Forms/C2118/14

WAR DIARY
or
INTELLIGENCE SUMMARY.
(Erase heading not required.)

Army Form C. 2118.

Place	Date	Hour	Summary of Events and Information	Remarks and references to Appendices
TRENCHES	30-12-17		Hostile Artillery & Machine Guns worried Vickers Guns fired intermittently throughout the night at following targets:- 2000 at a.7.a. 70.22. & a.8.c. 08.28. 200 " " t.6.b. 75.87 & t.66.80.20 Work continued at all positions. Casualties 1 O.R. wounded.	
TRENCHES	31-12-17		Hostile Artillery & Machine Guns active to 25° & 26° below. Received some attention. Indirect fire carried out at following:- 150 rounds to a.7.c. 48.05.6 a.7.c. 80.28 200 " " a.7.a. 70.22 " a.8.c. 08.28 Emplacements, Tracks, & dug-outs improved	

J Sharpeid
Lieut.

Copy No............

47th M.G. Coy. OPERATION ORDER. No. 107.

20:12:1917.

1. — 47th M.G. Coy will relieve 49th M.G. Company in the Left Sector during the night 21/22nd inst.

2. — "A" Section will relieve Teams at Gun Positions Nos 21-24 (both inclusive).
"B" Section will relieve Teams at Gun Positions Nos 25-28 (both inclusive).
"C" Section will relieve Teams at Gun Positions Nos 29-32 (both inclusive).
"D" Section will relieve Teams at Gun Positions Nos 17-20 (both inclusive).
The Team at No. 28 Gun Positions will be attached to "C" Section.

3. — Guns and Spare Parts only will be taken into Line. All other Gun Kit will be taken over from the relieved Company.

4. — Section Officers will ensure that at least one man from each team knows the route to Company H.Q.

5. — As soon as Relief is complete, N.C.Os. will instruct Teams thoroughly in all orders relating to Gun Position in which they are.

6. — Ration and Transport arrangements have been notified. Tea Rations will be carried by the Relieving Teams.

7. Completion of Relief will be notified to Company H.Q.

C.B. Hale, Captain.
Commanding
No. 47. M.G. Coy

Copy No 1. — C.O.
2. — 2nd in Command.
3. — T.O.
4. — O.C. "A" Section.
5. — O.C. "B" Section.
6. — O.C. "C" Section.
7. — O.C. "D" Section.
8. and 9. War Diary
10. — Office.

WAR DIARY

FOR MONTH OF JANUARY, 1918.

VOLUME :- 22

UNIT :- 47th Machine Gun Coy. M.G.C.

WAR DIARY
or
INTELLIGENCE SUMMARY.

(Erase heading not required.)

Army Form C. 2118.

H/14th M.G. Coy.
M.G.C.

Instructions regarding War Diaries and Intelligence Summaries are contained in F. S. Regs., Part II. and the Staff Manual respectively. Title pages will be prepared in manuscript.

Place	Date	Hour	Summary of Events and Information	Remarks and references to Appendices
TRENCHES	1-1-18		Putting of importance, and all quiet apart from Live Guns fired 5,00 rounds on Stand Junctions intermittently throughout night. Lewis at all points continued.	
TRENCHES	2-1-18		Usual activity. No part of Enemy. Coy relieved by strength as per O.O. 108 attached	
TINCOURT	3-1-18		Coy party holiday during morning. Cleaning up of kit & Equipment.	
TINCOURT	4-1-18		Kit, arms & checked. Inspection of S.B.R. & P.H. Helmets & spare rations. Lecture at F.U.C.A. Hut Tincourt in afternoon. (Map Reading)	

J. Gaspell Lieut

Army Form C. 2118.

WAR DIARY
or
INTELLIGENCE SUMMARY.
(Erase heading not required.)

Instructions regarding War Diaries and Intelligence Summaries are contained in F. S. Regs., Part II. and the Staff Manual respectively. Title pages will be prepared in manuscript.

Place	Date	Hour	Summary of Events and Information	Remarks and references to Appendices
TINCOURT	5-1-18		COs inspection. Elementary M.G. instruction. Lecture at Y.M.C.A. in afternoon.	
TINCOURT	6-1-18		Checking of Lewis Guns, Gun pits & List of deficiencies attended. Lecture as on previous days.	
TINCOURT	7-1-18		Company Drill & Elementary M.G. instruction during morning. 2.30 p.m. Lecture in Y.M.C.A.	
TINCOURT	8-1-18		Immediate Action & Cases of Stoppages. 10.30 a.m. & 12-0 noon Route March. Route:- BOIS du BOIRE – MONT ROUGE – BOIRE – TINCOURT. 2.30 p.m. Transport Inspection parade.	

J. Satfield
Lieut

Army Form C. 2118.

WAR DIARY
or
INTELLIGENCE SUMMARY.
(Erase heading not required.)

Place	Date	Hour	Summary of Events and Information	Remarks and references to Appendices
TINCOURT	9=1=18		Small Box Respirator Drill. Coach Machine Gun Training 2-30 p.m. Lecture in Y.M.C.A. (Maj Pinking)	
TINCOURT	10=1=18	9-15 a.m. to 12.00 noon preparing & cleaning of Guns for the Limbers, picked in preparation for Relief. No 10 Section Advanceurs in forward Pits and Equipment Completed. All Officers Reconnaitre Right Sector.	
TINCOURT	11=1=18	S.B.R. & P.H. Helmet inspection Guns Lifted 1-30 p.m. Company paraded in fighting Gear for the Line. # 9 M.G. Coy Relief in Right Sector. Relief Completed by 6-30 p.m.	
TRENCHES	12=1=18		Enemy activity has ceased to Hostile Artillery fire during night. Guns fired on selected Targets behind enemy front System during night — Zero rounds being expended.	J Stanfield Lieut

Army Form C. 2118.

WAR DIARY
or
INTELLIGENCE SUMMARY.
(Erase heading not required.)

Place	Date	Hour	Summary of Events and Information	Remarks and references to Appendices
TRENCHES	13-1-18		Enemy Artillery more than usual - Entirely good. This Accounted for increased activity on part of Enemy Artillery & aircraft. 1,600 rounds were fired by our left at Hostile Aircraft.	
			At 9.15 a.m. 3 E.A. crossed our lines, & were engaged by A.A. & M.G. in Gun Fire. One Enemy Machine was brought down in our lines the pilot being killed. Another E.A. was seen to fall in Enemy lines.	
			At 3.45 p.m. an Enemy TRIPLANE succeeded in destroying one of our Balloons but was eventually followed & brought down by A.A. & M.G. & ll action gun fire. The pilot was captured.	
			Our Guns fired 5,600 rounds during night on hostile targets in Enemy Front & support lines. Work continued. Meeting enemy position.	

J Stafford
Lieut

Army Form C. 2118.

WAR DIARY
or
INTELLIGENCE SUMMARY.
(Erase heading not required.)

Place	Date	Hour	Summary of Events and Information	Remarks and references to Appendices
TRENCHES	14-1-18		Enemy Artillery quiet. Nothing of importance to report from Lieu. Guns fired 6,650 rounds in C.T's. Gun's position throughout night. Work at all positions continued.	
TRENCHES	15-1-18		Hostile activity active. Dug-outs in HOSTAR ROAD hit heavily. Shelled for about 15 minutes at 8 p.m. Vickers Guns Harassing fire intermittently throughout night to following targets. — BONY TRENCH — 2,700 rounds A 20.2.06.75: — 2,650 " A 20.2.70.00 — 2,700 " 2, no " Lost cross rd at Enemy position, kept at 11.9.12 - ft. arctic.	J. Shattuck Lieut
TRENCHES	16-1-18		Hostile Artillery normally active. Vickers gun harassing fire as follows. — BONY AVENUE 3,650 rounds A.20.a.70.00. 2, no "	

WAR DIARY
or
INTELLIGENCE SUMMARY.

Army Form C. 2118.

Place	Date	Hour	Summary of Events and Information	Remarks and references to Appendices
TRENCHES	16-1-18	(cont'd)	Artillery very hostile owing to rain & our Arty. work. Drawing on our lines.	
TRENCHES	17-1-18		Hostile Artillery normal. Between 2-20 pm & 4-0 pm enemy shelled Kr 5 & 6 positions & Craullin. Our guns fired intermittently throughout eight following targets:	
			BONY AVENUE — 5,650 rounds
			SUNKEN ROAD — 5,000 "
			(Ap 2.2.70.53)
			At P2. 05.35. 1,650 "
			L.S.R. continued as Esplanaments, Haunts, Dugouts & Rovers positions.	
TRENCHES	18-1-18		Hostile Artillery & Machine Gun action Kr 6, 9 & 10 positions. Weak concentration. Harasst fire carried at 2 fellows. BONY AVENUE 9000 rounds. SUNKEN ROAD, 1,650 rounds. St Stratford trench	

Army Form C. 2118.

WAR DIARY
or
INTELLIGENCE SUMMARY.
(Erase heading not required.)

Place	Date	Hour	Summary of Events and Information	Remarks and references to Appendices
TRENCHES	18-1-18		H.9.c.05.35 to H.9.d.45.55 2,000 rounds. No culminate at all points	
TRENCHES	19-1-18		Lewis Artillery & Machine Gun action. Aircraft action away evening. 2,000 rounds fired at enemy aircraft. One gun fired at points:- CLAYMORE TRENCH 1,750 rounds PONY AVENUE 2,000 " SUNKEN ROAD 5,000 " H.20.a.9.c. H.7.b.75.55 to H.7.b.75.30 1,600 " Lab. Enemy trench & Artillery Fire.	
TRENCHES	20-1-18		Hostile Artillery & M.G. ie Gun Action. On account of Heavy Artillery Bombardment on neighbour gun fired at dos aic to Co.S. Line (6-15 am) Vickers Guns fired 6,000 rounds as noted N.F. targets	

Army Form C. 2118.

WAR DIARY
or
INTELLIGENCE SUMMARY.
(Erase heading not required.)

Place	Date	Hour	Summary of Events and Information	Remarks and references to Appendices
TRENCHES	21-1-18		Hostile Artillery/Machine Gun. Found activity. One of our guns fired on the following target during the night:- A.I.d.10.90. X ROADS DIRK ALLEY BONY AVENUE 2000 rounds 1,000 " 1,000 " L.M.Gs continued with Staff, bursts & emplacements	
TRENCHES	22-1-18		Hostile Artillery & Aircraft. Active Transport point Vicinity of Coy H.Q shelled during afternoon. A large proportion being gas shells. E.A. 15 & 16 prowled around. Came & attacked. 2,500 rounds fired at hostile aircraft. Vickers Guns fired on the following high intermittently during the night. CLAYMORE AVENUE 1,500 rounds BONY AVENUE 1,500 " A.I.d.10.90. 1,500 " L.M.K Coulumn J Hatfield Lieut	

WAR DIARY
or
INTELLIGENCE SUMMARY

Army Form C. 2118.

Place	Date	Hour	Summary of Events and Information	Remarks and references to Appendices
TRENCHES	23-1-18		Hostile Artillery & Machine Gun work actively. 4 Officers of A.P.O.R. 9th 269 M.G. Coy sent into Right Sector for instruction. Indirect fire carried out as follows:—	
			d.g.c. 65°35' f. A.8.C. 46'35 (Shooting fine)	1,650 rounds
			CLAYMORE AVENUE	1,650 "
			BONY AVENUE	1,650 "
			Considerable fog — no shots made with Expt. Amp. A.S.	
TRENCHES	24-1-18		Hostile Artillery active throughout period. O.K. 5.9" & 4.2" on 10.5cm. Gas Shells fired into ENEMY Hostile M.G. active from X.27 c.4.7	
			Our Guns fired on the following targets intermittently throughout night:—	
			M.I.A. 10.90	1,650 rds.
			CLAYMORE AVENUE	1,650 rds.
			BONY LANE	1,650 rds.

Army Form C. 2118.

WAR DIARY
or
INTELLIGENCE SUMMARY.
(Erase heading not required.)

Place	Date	Hour	Summary of Events and Information	Remarks and references to Appendices
TRENCHES	25-1-18		Hostile Aircraft active. Artillery & Machine Guns normal. 1.9.55 Trench was fired at by E.A. during day. Indirect fire carried out as follows:— CLAYMORE AVENUE 2000 rds BONY AVENUE 2000 rds F1.85.05.35 & F1.85.45.55 2000 rds (Verdun) 3 officers & 4 8 O.R. sent with Regt Sectn for instruction with Lefts Any-al.	
TRENCHES	26-1-18		Hostile Artillery normal. Vickers Guns fired as follows intermittently throughout night. A 20.C. 01: 92 1,500 rounds A. 14.C. 35: 22 1,500 " H. 20.C. 01: 92 1,500 " H. 14.C. 35: 22 1,500 " F.C. & NEW YORK 1,500 " A 8.C.05:35 & F1.8.C.45:55 1,500 " Work continued.	

Army Form C. 2118.

WAR DIARY
or
INTELLIGENCE SUMMARY.
(Erase heading not required.)

Instructions regarding War Diaries and Intelligence Summaries are contained in F. S. Regs., Part II. and the Staff Manual respectively. Title pages will be prepared in manuscript.

Place	Date	Hour	Summary of Events and Information	Remarks and references to Appendices
TRENCHES	27-1-18		Hostile Artillery. Machine Gun & small arms gun fire at
Yellow –
A.14.C. 35.22 — 1,650 rounds
F.6.d. TIGER & TOM BOIS. Trs. 1,170 rounds
A.14.d. 09.61 — 1650 rounds
A.14.c. 69.55 — 1650 rounds
Look out continued brisk shafts & sinf. arc	JR
TRENCHES	28-1-18		Hostile Artillery. Machine Gun's arrived. Wicker Gun
feed intermittently throughout the night on the
Supervisory lines.
A.20.c. 35.75 — 1650
A.14.c. 36.22 — 1,650
A.20.c. 46.86 — 1,650
A.14.c. 25.21 — 1,650
A.8.c. 65.35 — 1,120
A.8.c. 45.55 — 1,765
F.6.d. TIGER & TOM BOIS.Trs — 1,000
& H.E. Continued	Shortfifth Lieut

Army Form C. 2118.

WAR DIARY
or
INTELLIGENCE SUMMARY
(Erase heading not required.)

Instructions regarding War Diaries and Intelligence Summaries are contained in F.S. Regs., Part II. and the Staff Manual respectively. Title pages will be prepared in manuscript.

Hour, Date, Place	Summary of Events and Information	Remarks and references to Appendices
TRENCHES 29-1-18	Company relieved in line by 26gth Coy. Relief complete by 5-30 p.m. On completion of relief Coy returned to Billets at VILLERS FAUCON.	
VILLERS FAUCON 30-1-18	Parades. General clean up & cooking of kit off. 2-30 p.m. pay parade.	
VILLERS FAUCON 31-1-18	Parades. Constructing Anti Aircraft protection. Cleaning Guns, & Gun equipment.	

J. Stopper Lieut.

WAR DIARY.

FOR MONTH OF FEBRUARY, 1918.

VOLUME:-

UNIT:- 47th Machine Gun Company.

No. 47. Machine Gun Coy.

WAR DIARY
- for -
FEBRUARY - 1918.

47TH M. G. COY.
No. W.D.II.
Date 1918

Army Form C. 2118.

WAR DIARY
or
INTELLIGENCE SUMMARY.
(Erase heading not required.)

Instructions regarding War Diaries and Intelligence Summaries are contained in F. S. Regs., Part II. and the Staff Manual respectively. Title pages will be prepared in manuscript.

Place	Date	Hour	Summary of Events and Information	Remarks and references to Appendices
VILLERS FAUCON	1-2-18		Parade. 9-15 a.m. C.O.P. Inspection. 9-30 " 10-15 a.m. Physical Training. 10-15 " 11-noon. Arms Drill. 11-30 " 12-30 p.m. Squad & Company drill. 2-10 p.m. to 3.00 p.m. Lecture.	
VILLERS FAUCON	2-2-18		Parade. 9-15 a.m. to 10-15 a.m. Physical Training. 10-15 a.m. to 12-30 p.m. Elementary Drill & Protective movements by Officers & N.C.O.s and S.A.A. M.T.L.I.E.	
VILLERS FAUCON	3-2-18		Parade. Church parade. Rador practice. Cleaning of Arms & Rifles.	

Army Form C. 2118.

WAR DIARY
or
INTELLIGENCE SUMMARY.
(Erase heading not required.)

Instructions regarding War Diaries and Intelligence Summaries are contained in F. S. Regs., Part II. and the Staff Manual respectively. Title pages will be prepared in manuscript.

Place	Date	Hour	Summary of Events and Information	Remarks and references to Appendices
VILLERS FAUCON	4-2-18	Parade	9-15 am & 10-15 am Company Drill. 10-15 am & 12-30 pm Advanced Drill Company Visual training. 2-00 pm to 3-00 pm Lecture.	
VILLERS FAUCON	5-2-18	Parade	9-15 am Coy Inspection. 9-30 am & 10-15 am Physical Drill. 10-15 am & 11-0 am Company Drill. 11-30 am & 12-30 pm Cleaning Guns & Kit, preparing for Relief.	
VILLERS FAUCON	6-2-18	Parade	9-30am to 12-30pm Fighting Order. 10-30 am & 12-30 pm prepare Guns for line. 4-15 pm Coy moved off for line & relieved H Bull Coy Left Section Reliefs completed by 5-30 pm. Right Quiet.	

Army Form C. 2118.

WAR DIARY
or
INTELLIGENCE SUMMARY.

(Erase heading not required.)

Instructions regarding War Diaries and Intelligence Summaries are contained in F. S. Regs., Part II. and the Staff Manual respectively. Title pages will be prepared in manuscript.

Place	Date	Hour	Summary of Events and Information	Remarks and references to Appendices
TRENCHES	7-2-18.		Active Artillery & Machine Gun & Trench mortar. Snipers & Guns but not yet no account of our patrols sent out at all positions.	
TRENCHES	8-2-18.		Active Artillery normal. Machine Guns active at night. Ret 17+18 patrols worked around EAGLE QUARRY, our Guns around & Enemy actively firing intermittently throughout the night. Working on staff at 20 to 28 positions. Much ammunition, & Trench mortar at all positions.	
TRENCHES	9-2-18.		Active Artillery fairly active. RIDGE RESERVE TRENCH, MAH COPSE & EPEHY worked same actively. Our Guns fired 2 no rounds at LOWLAND POST (17.6.82.) intermittently throughout the night. Patrols covered at 25 22 23 positions. Patrols continued with slaughtering weapons & trenches	J. Stafford Lieut

WAR DIARY or INTELLIGENCE SUMMARY

Army Form C. 2118.

Place	Date	Hour	Summary of Events and Information	Remarks and references to Appendices
TRENCHES	10-2-18.		HOSTILE ARTILLERY active. RIDGE RESERVE TRENCH, & vicinity of HAY CORSE shelled intermittently throughout evening. Fritz 10.5 c.m. and 15 c.m. Hostile machine guns fired short bursts during night & early morning over F.3.c. and F.9.b. Enemy Aircraft. One E.A. Albros, one two seater at 10 pm flying low engaged back by A.A. fire 250 rounds fired at this E.A. by H.A. M.G. Flash of an enemy gun observed at a bearing of 320° TRUE from F.10.c.46.55. A few Red Very light signals observed during night in Left Sector. On account of active patrolling of No Mans Land only six flare or Verey lights no (Harper) H.7.b.2.5. fired 12.30 a.m. 6 to 7 a.m. Look outwards at all positions. Hostile artillery active throughout day. Especially between 1-0 p.m. & 4-0 p.m. MALASSISE FARM & TEDHARD WOOD accessed. Enemy bombardment on Right Front your position 5.30 pm	
TRENCHES	11-2-18.			

Army Form C. 2118.

WAR DIARY
or
INTELLIGENCE SUMMARY.
(Erase heading not required.)

Instructions regarding War Diaries and Intelligence Summaries are contained in F.S. Regs., Part II. and the Staff Manual respectively. Title pages will be prepared in manuscript.

Place	Date	Hour	Summary of Events and Information	Remarks and references to Appendices
TRENCHES	11.2.18		Cault. With usual Calibre Hostile Machine Gun fired short bursts over Pts 27 & 30 during night. Hostile Guns. During bombardment by our guns 4.30 p.m. to 5.20 p.m. Given answered light hostile shrapnel fire at our rail & S.F. lines. Gas alarm sounded at LOWLAND POST during night but continued at all points.	
TRENCHES	12.2.18.		Hostile Artillery normal. Machine Gun active between 6-0 p.m. & 7-0 p.m. Aircraft active. Searchlight seen operated behind enemy front system from 5:20 p.m. to 6:15 p.m. Chain lights were given after dark. Our Green fired 200 rounds at LOWLAND POST and vicinity intermittently throughout night. Jacobs Augsb. Inspected. J Stratford Lieut	

D.D. & L. London. — Avon.) Wt. 17714/2031 795m'oo 5/17 Sch. 52 Forms C2116/4

Army Form C. 2118.

WAR DIARY
or
INTELLIGENCE SUMMARY.
(Erase heading not required.)

Place	Date	Hour	Summary of Events and Information	Remarks and references to Appendices
TRENCHES	13-2-18		Hostile Artillery quiet. Machine Guns active LEMPIRE, EAST of Gen. H.Q. (F.10.e.76.45) Round attention. Vickers Guns 2010 rounds fired at intervals through night at EAGLE QUARRY. Various coloured lights sent up by enemy during night & early morning. Lights - 1 shrapnel two shrapnel over a Lewis gun post F.10.e.5.5.55. 2nd Lieutenant [signature]	
TRENCHES	14-2-18.		Hostile Artillery active. The following targets [?] place were engaged. LEMPIRE, RONSSOY, 5 PENY F.9.d & F.10.c. Hostile Trench Works at Oak 12-0 midnight & 12.20 a.m. 20 Gravenstafel Bombs were fired into front line of Left Sector. Vickers Guns Fired B. F.5.c.65.22. (TOMBOIS VALLEY) 3000 rounds suspected enemy relief	J. Stafford Lieut

WAR DIARY
INTELLIGENCE SUMMARY.

Army Form C. 2118.

Place	Date	Hour	Summary of Events and Information	Remarks and references to Appendices
TRENCHES	15-2-18.		Hostile Artillery unusual. Trench Mortars, Grenades. Very TMs fell near LITTLE PRIEL FARM between 5.30 p.m. & 8.05 p.m. Hostile Machine Guns moderately active at intervals during day & night. At 10.30 p.m. Vint at point F.9.c.15.92 raided by M.G. also M.H.HOUSE ROAD and left of RAILWAY POST. He firing of 2 enemy M.G.s was traced F.15.b.82.30. direction 19° & 28°. TMs look continued on Staff & Trenches.	J.L.
TRENCHES	16-2-18.		Hostile Artillery unusual. Machine Guns active & sniper F.9.c.15.92 received attention during night. Vickers Guns fired 8,000 rounds as S.O.S. in enemy line at LHOK. POST during night. Work continued.	J.L.
TRENCHES	17-2-18.		Hostile Artillery, Aircraft & Machine Gun – active. Vickers Guns fired intermittently throughout the night on points behind enemy front line.	

Army Form C. 2118.

WAR DIARY
or
INTELLIGENCE SUMMARY.
(Erase heading not required.)

Instructions regarding War Diaries and Intelligence Summaries are contained in F. S. Regs., Part II. and the Staff Manual respectively. Title pages will be prepared in manuscript.

Place	Date	Hour	Summary of Events and Information	Remarks and references to Appendices
TRENCHES	17-2-18		Cont. 2.00 a.m. to fired at enemy aircraft. Searchlights active until moonlight (N.9.5.P.E.H.). Sub continued.	
TRENCHES	18-2-18.		Hostile Artillery. Aircraft active visiting gun positions. Operations. Retired to camp for day. Lewis guns fired intermittently throughout night. Lewis guns fired 6 p.m. & 12.20 p.m. Road out of up gun emplacement. It appears that the enemy sent to find out our G.P. signal. Search lights were active at intervals during night. Staffs: trenches, Vierzy, 8.* Took contained belt.	
TRENCHES	19-2-18.		At 4-00 a.m. attacked by artillery. Lasted gun 80 yards. Military see company fired two enemy letter carved in H. 7. Sparkle encountered 6 prisoners. The Machine guns kept it in the line kept spending.	

D D & I., London, E.C. (A'oo) W.t. W 17/M5031 750000 5/17 Sch. 52 Forms C2. a/4

WAR DIARY
or
INTELLIGENCE SUMMARY.

Army Form C. 2118.

Place	Date	Hour	Summary of Events and Information	Remarks and references to Appendices
TRENCHES	19-2-18		Quiet. Night, and support gun & rail at 4 a.m. Gas alert experienced. Hostile Machine gun active N. of Epéhy. Aircraft active on both sides. Our own airplane too close sub. of Epéhy were BOMY one of our machines was attacked by 5 E.A. which drove her down near TOMBOIS FARM, and fell in F.10.a. Work continued.	[signature]
TRENCHES	20-2-18		Quiet. Artillery active, LEMPIRE, RONSSOY, EPEHY accounted for. Hostile Machine guns active. Our gun M.Gun in front of attention. Lewis Machine guns 20,22 & 23 F.9.c. Victor guns Work. 3 no rounds during night at MAC.Q.VINCOURT. VALLEY supplies laying tr. Several that Enemy actively at work taking the early work continued with Staff, Trench, & Emplacements	[signature] Lieut.

Army Form C. 2118.

WAR DIARY
or
INTELLIGENCE SUMMARY.
(Erase heading not required.)

Place	Date	Hour	Summary of Events and Information	Remarks and references to Appendices
TRENCHES	21-2-18		Hostile Artillery Active between 4-30 a.m. to 6-30 a.m. Enemy barraged CATELET VALLEY with all calibre. Also M.G. Guns opening rate effort seemed for at A.D.S. during Relievin(?). Gun fire in unusually (?) Capt. Fee A.M.C, Chy Sgnt Perry wounded, Rfm Stopard 3560, Rfm Brown 412517 Lee Corp Lind Pearceater (?) of day quiet.	J S
TRENCHES	22-2-18		Hostile Artillery Normal. Aircraft active during morning. Vickers Gun Carried out the usual harassing fire during night on Enemy C.T's, & track. Saw several of E.H. during retirement. At 7-10 p.m. an explosion took place in (rear of) Sheep Lines (Isolation TREE NORTH) from F.15.a.6.0.90	J S
TRENCHES	23-2-18		Hostile Artillery unusual. Hostile Machine Guns active. E-Le Pouvre Yser Canal QUARRY Fisselles from Lab Catechism at all points.	J Stratford Lieut

Army Form C. 2118.

WAR DIARY
or
INTELLIGENCE SUMMARY.
(Erase heading not required.)

Place	Date	Hour	Summary of Events and Information	Remarks and references to Appendices
TRENCHES	24-2-18		Hostile Artillery active 4 Hyres & B-M on EMPIRE & RONSOY intermittently. Hostile Machine Guns were active during night. Our Artillery active with HA guns also harassing fire on TNGE heavy N.S.T. front A.P.C. 34-65. Believed to be in area of Cross Roads in K24.c. Work continued.	K
TRENCHES	25-2-18		Hostile Artillery active EMPIRE. RONSOY & PSHY accural attention. Hostile Machine Guns active throughout night. Hostile Aircraft active visibility being good, 1,500 rounds fired at EA during period. Our Machine Gun fire live on fire, many K "Highlight point" being out. Work continued.	K
TRENCHES	26-2-18		Hostile Artillery, Machine Guns active. Enemy aeroplane fired on EAGLE QUARRY. Machine Gun active upon EAGLE QUARRY. Enemy Aeroplane shot down near Yssipees trent	

Army Form C. 2118.

WAR DIARY
or
INTELLIGENCE SUMMARY.
(Erase heading not required.)

Instructions regarding War Diaries and Intelligence Summaries are contained in F. S. Regs., Part II. and the Staff Manual respectively. Title pages will be prepared in manuscript.

Place	Date	Hour	Summary of Events and Information	Remarks and references to Appendices
TRENCHES	26-2-16		Ould. Quiet morning. Enemy MG direct hit on Station HQ (F.15.a.30.6.0.) Casualties 1 officer wounded. 2 Lt R.J. WEBB. Work carried out all position.	J Shuttleworth Lieut

WAR DIARY
or
INTELLIGENCE SUMMARY.

Army Form C. 2118.

(Erase heading not required.)

Place	Date	Hour	Summary of Events and Information	Remarks and references to Appendices
TRENCHES	26/6/2018		Relieved 3 pm & 4th Jan. Took over line engaged by 5RR. Anti aircraft M.G.F. Work continued, Lill. Shefts, Emplacements & Tracks.	J.
TRENCHES	27-7-18		Mobile Artillery Active. At 11.45 p.m. heavy bombardment in front of Dinnen in sight. At 12.5 am S.O.S. for Our Guns. Enemy light; opened fire on G.F. line. Hostile Aircraft active Away from vicinity gnd. 10. Enemy howitzer blew up during day. Vicker Gun fired 1000 Round at E.A. during day. Work continued at M.C. position.	J.
TRENCHES	28-7-18		Hostile Artillery Active. H.V & T.M.S slight activity GRAFTON POST Direct collision Trench Mor.	Maurice Leak

woe57/1971 (5)

woe57/1971 (5)

~~2 ARMY~~

16 DIV 47 Bde
47

TRENCH MORTAR
BTY

1915 NOV to 1915 DEC

(1682)

WAR DIARY
or
INTELLIGENCE SUMMARY
(Erase heading not required.)

Army Form C. 2118

4 Trench Mortar [signature]

Place	Date	Hour	Summary of Events and Information	Remarks and references to Appendices
Armagh Wood	9/11/15		Day spent in looking for good gun emplacements & in making 2" mortar emplacement & bomb store for mortar bombs. owing to heavy enemy front line fire in several places all night no wiring was done.	
"	10/11/15		Fired 4 rounds 4" mortar at working party observed at I.30.c.73 the being only gun mortar. Enemy retaliated during enemy, but our fire had succeeded in reducing their working party.	
"	11/11/15		Fired 2 rounds 4" mortar at I.29.D.96 for registration	
"	12/11/15		Time spent repairing emplacements etc; no rounds fired.	
"	13/11/15		Fired 5 rounds 2" mortar from emplacement I.30.9.2½ at enemies trenches between I.29.D.37 & I.29.D.96. one 2" mortar fired, & forward mortar were in action + 16 rounds were fired on enemies trenches between I.29.D.37 & I.29.D.85. All rounds appeared to be successful in reaching their object. Relief took place to-day.	
"	14/11/15		Day spent in repairing emplacements which had been damaged by heavy rain.	
"	15/11/15		Arrangements were made with the Artillery to fire on the afternoon of the 16th at enemy emplacement got in readiness.	
"	16/11/15		Fired 16 rounds 4" mortars from 2 guns at enemies trenches at I.29.D.9.5 from emplacement I.30.09.5 & I.30.C.9.½. One round fell short but rest were proved by observation to be good. & several breaches in enemies trenches were made.	
"	17/11/15		Day spent in preparing a new emplacement from which to engage strong point pointed out by machine gun officer.	
"	18/11/15		Day spent in arranging about for 19th inst. & relieving day out.	

[signature] 4 Aug 18 [illegible]

Army Form C. 2118

WAR DIARY
or
INTELLIGENCE SUMMARY
(Erase heading not required.)

Instructions regarding War Diaries and Intelligence Summaries are contained in F.S. Regs., Part II. and the Staff Manual respectively. Title Pages will be prepared in manuscript.

Place	Date	Hour	Summary of Events and Information	Remarks and references to Appendices
Through[out]	19/11/15		Fired 4 rounds 4" mortar from emplacement at I.30.C.51.7 at square of sandbags in enemy lines opposite to it as a machine gun emplacement. The erection was dismantled by first + 2nd round 3rd + 4th being blind. No fuzes in all cases were observed to be burning. The emplacement for 2" gun was blown in by shell fire + gun buried but not damaged.	
	20/11/15		Day spent repairing 2" emplacement + dug out. Gunner Haight 54879 R.G.A. was sent to hospital wounded, shell with self inflicted wound.	
	21/11/15		Officers dug out blown in by shell fire + had to be rebuilt. Officers relieved.	
	22/11/15		Officers dug out completed + things cleared up. 2" emplacement made in through wood.	
	23/11/15		then worked on communication trench parapet as ordered by Brigadier.	
	24/11/15		Men again worked on communication trench parapet.	
	25/11/15		Reliefs took place. Bomb store blown in + had to be replaced.	
	26/11/15		Bomb store finished + communication trench cleared.	
	27/11/15		New dug out blown in + 4 men buried one man slightly wounded. Dug out cleared of this etc + abandoned + a new one refused.	
	28/11/15		Built a new ammunition store for 2" bomb further 4" emplacement made near Hd Quarters.	
	29/11/15		Fired 11 rounds 4" mortar one gun only fired from emplacement at I.30.B.15 at strong point on enemy line I.30.D.39 at a range of 380 yds. 3 shells were observed although fuzes were seen burning. The remainder were seen to do great damage.	
	30/11/15		Inspection by G.O.C., C.R.E., T.D.O.C, T.S., Brigade, new 2" bomb store abandoned owing to dead body being found.	

WAR DIARY or INTELLIGENCE SUMMARY

Army Form C. 2118

Place	Date	Hour	Summary of Events and Information	Remarks and references to Appendices
Sanctuary Wood	1/12/15		Prepared emplacements for shoot on 2nd inst. Men engaged also on helping to build new canteen.	
"	2/12/15		Fired 6 rounds 2" mortar from emplacement at I30c6&0 at front in enemy lines I30c16, which is very effective burst the screen for the blinds and that the range was too short, also fired 14 rounds 4" on same target for emplacement I30A21 two blinds. The remainder very satisfactory with at least 2 direct hits. This shoot was in conjunction with the artillery & was most satisfactory. Relief took place. New Bomb store for 4" ammunition started, build the 4" defensive emplacement.	
"	3/12/15		Bomb store completed.	
"	4/12/15			
"	5/12/15		This day was spent on filling sandbags & digging out the position of new canteen in continuation of what was done on the 1st inst.	
"	6/12/15		Continued filling sandbags for canteen.	
"	7/12/15		Sandbags put in position.	
"	8/12/15		Joined the with 4.5 Howitzers in bombardment on front I30B40 with one 4" & one 2" gun firing. 4 rounds fired from 2" & 4 rounds from 4" after 4th round 2" strained perceivably & was out of action. The 4" fired very successfully 2nd shot forming just outside the practically 2nd shot fired under same conditions hitting the target which our own parapet. The 3rd shot fired under same conditions hitting the target while the 4" the shot burst just over the parapet again.	
"	9/12/15		Relief took place this day. 2" repaired & made again put in action.	Jackson Capt R.A. Comdg 171 T.M.B.

1875 Wt. W593/826 1,000,000 4/15 J.B.C. & A. A.D.S.S./Forms/C.2118.

Army Form C. 2118

WAR DIARY
or
INTELLIGENCE SUMMARY
(Erase heading not required.)

Instructions regarding War Diaries and Intelligence Summaries are contained in F. S. Regs., Part II. and the Staff Manual respectively. Title Pages will be prepared in manuscript.

Place	Date	Hour	Summary of Events and Information	Remarks and references to Appendices
Armentières	10/12/15		men again on making canteen.	
	11/12/15		2" gun emplacement fell in where 0.2 fires the gun from this was repaired.	
	12/12/15		communication trench to 2" gun observed & duck boarded in parts.	
	13/12/15		2" gun emplacement was altered so as to enable Target I 30 C 08 to be engaged.	
	14/12/15		4" emplacement at point I 30 B 33½ made & telephone were laid from 2" gun at Twist I 30 C 22.0 to our trench A1.	
	15/12/15		Fired 20 rounds 4" from one gun position I 30 B 33½ at enemies Trenches D. 7 direct hits were observed – much damage done & lot of timber being seen in the air at I 30 C 08. Of the remaining shells 3 were blind the others did damage in German Trenches behind front line.	
	16/12/15		2" gun fired 9 rounds from I 30 A 2½.0 at enemies Trenches I 29 D 37 seven shells were seen to tell & the bursts were satisfactory in or just behind the Target. 3 rounds 4" were fired at German dug outs at I 29 D 85 – two were seen to tell, one was unobserved. 4" fired from I 30 A 21. Reliefs took place.	
	17/12/15		Collected & made inventory of all stores in the Trenches.	

1875 Wt. W593/826 1,000,000 4/15 J.B.C. & A. A.D.S.S./Forms/C.2118.

Army Form C. 2118

WAR DIARY
or
INTELLIGENCE SUMMARY
(Erase heading not required.)

Place	Date	Hour	Summary of Events and Information	Remarks and references to Appendices
Army(?)amp	19/10/15		Conducted relieving officer 50th Div round Trenches, carried out sniping shooting Sanctuary Wood.	
	20/10/15		Stood to at 4.30 A.M. & continued to do so until 7 A.M. on 20th inst when Battery was relieved by the 50th Div T.M. Battery.	

Robert Onyjal(?) Capt.
27 T.M.B.